DELUSIONS OF

JOHN RAE has been described
and controversial figures in the
During his long headmastership of Westminster School,
1970–1986, he became the best-known headmaster of his
time, partly because he took an independent line on a
number of educational issues and partly because he used
the media skilfully to put across his ideas. John Rae was
elected chairman of the Headmasters Conference in1977.

In a varied and colourful life, John Rae has played
rugby for London Scottish, worked in an Indian leper
village, helped in the making of the film *The Killing
Fields*, written, broadcast and appeared on television.
When he left Westminster in 1986, he became the first
director of the Laura Ashley Foundation. In 1989, he was
appointed director of the Portman Group, a body set up
by the UK drinks industry to combat alcohol misuse. His
previous books are *Letters from School* (1987) and *Too
Little, Too Late?* (1989). He and his wife Daphne have
four daughters and unidentical twin sons, all of whom are
grown up. They also now have seven grandchildren. John
Rae lives in London.

Delusions of Grandeur

A Headmaster's Life
1966–1986

JOHN RAE

HarperCollins*Publishers*

HarperCollins*Publishers*
77–85 Fulham Palace Road,
Hammersmith, London W6 8JB

This paperback edition 1994
1 3 5 7 9 8 6 4 2

First published in Great Britain by
HarperCollins*Publishers* 1993

ISBN 0 00 638129 4

The publishers wish to thank Methuen Children's Books
for permission to quote from 'King John's Christmas' in
Now We Are Six by A.A. Milne, and Basic Books Inc. for the
excerpt from *Preparing for Power* by Peter W. Cookson Jr
and Carolyn Hodges Persell.

Set in Linotron Janson

Printed in Great Britain by
HarperCollinsManufacturing Glasgow

To my Granddaughter

HANNAH

*who refused to stand up when the teacher
entered until someone explained
why she should*

'Even the best head is going to make some enemies, and in the final analysis even the most successful head is expendable. The ever-present fact of life for the head is that he or she is vulnerable, a condition not conducive to peace of mind or relaxation. To be seen as defeated can cause a decrease in credibility, and at some point charisma can turn to catastrophe if a head loses his or her special authority. Yet, by nature most heads are adaptive and conservative, and adroit at diffusing disaster. Their survival instincts are generally advanced.'

Peter W. Cookson and Caroline Hodges Persell, *Preparing for Power: America's Elite Boarding Schools*, 1985

CONTENTS

FOREWORD

The aim of this book is to explore, through my own experience, the role of the English public school headmaster: his public and his private face; his outward confidence and inward fears; his use and abuse of his unusual power; his battle to reform or just to keep control of the school; his relations with his staff and with his pupils; his pursuit of fame and his delusions of grandeur. There are biographies and autobiographies of headmasters, but they do not tell you much about what it is really like to do the job. Fiction has been more successful in entering the headmaster's mind. I am not thinking of the most famous case, Thomas Hughes's portrait of Dr Arnold in *Tom Brown's Schooldays*, but of a more recent and less well-known novel, *The Rector of Justin* by Louis Auchincloss. Other novelists have tried to create or recreate the character of a headmaster; sometimes he is at the centre of the novel as in Anthony Trollope's *Dr Wortle's School* or G. F. Bradby's *The Lanchester Tradition*; sometimes he is a supporting player as in Samuel Butler's *The Way of all Flesh* (an unflattering portrait of Butler's own headmaster at Shrewsbury) or Hugh Walpole's *Mr Perrin and Mr Traill*. But Auchincloss is the only author who understands how the master's personality influences the way he will play the role *and* how the demands of the role draw out particular aspects of his personality. 'It is hard on the personality to be a headmaster,' says the Rector of Justin, a New England public school in the English style, 'it develops all my tendencies to strut and bully.'

Anyone who has been a public school headmaster will recognize the truth of that. What makes the life of a public school headmaster interesting is not just how he did the job but what the job did to him.

The English public schools, or independent schools as they prefer to be called, are like little kingdoms. Most of them are wholly or partly residential communities. They are self-governing. They have proud histories and entrenched traditions. To the outsider, their ancient buildings and rituals and their apparent detachment from the world may suggest Ruritania or Lilliput rather than a real country, but to the insiders the analogy of a kingdom is accurate enough.

The public school headmaster exercises personal power to a greater degree than many people in positions of authority. It is neither absolute nor unfettered power: a headmaster can be dismissed by the governing body that appointed him and his plans may be frustrated by his senior colleagues who, like medieval barons, combine against him. But a determined headmaster who is politically astute is difficult to dislodge and dangerous to oppose.

In recent times the arbitrary, even tyrannical, nature of the headmaster's power has been played down. Today's public school headmaster wishes to be seen as a chief executive not as an autocrat, but it is a change of style not of substance.

One man's experience cannot give a complete insight into the psychology of the public school autocrat. All I can do is describe what the job is like from the inside and hope that my autobiographical account rings as true as Louis Auchincloss's fictional.

For thirteen of my sixteen years as headmaster of Westminister School I kept a journal, writing down at the end of each day the events and my reactions to them. If my recollections of what people said and did, and of my thoughts and feelings, seem too precise to be true, it is because I have taken the information straight from my journal.

CHAPTER 1

Contradictions

My older brother, Angus, was the maverick of the family; I was the conformist. While I trimmed my sails to the wind, he would press on into the teeth of the storm. Such defiance may have been as much of a cover-up for insecurity as my cautious tacking but it caught the eye. Aunts and uncles who found me rather dull and difficult to fathom would greet his arrival in the room with cries of 'Here's Angus!' They cast him in the role of jester and, like an actor trapped in a long-running farce, it took him years to shed a reputation for recklessness.

An incident that occurred in 1940, when I was nine years old, appears at first sight to be out of character. One Sunday after lunch, just as my father was settling down in his armchair, I took a ripe plum from a bowl on the sideboard and left the house by the back door. A war-reserve policeman in his uniform was walking by on the other side of the road. I threw the plum at him and, by one of those flukes it is impossible to repeat, the plum hit him smack on the cheek bone and burst open. As he started across the road towards me, I ran back into the house. At the open door of the drawing room, I said, 'Daddy, there's a policeman to see you.' My father was splendid. What was all the fuss about? I was only a child. The policeman should be thankful the plum had not stained his brand new uniform.

My father never mentioned the incident again and it is only now, as I recall the details fifty years later, that I realize how pleased he must have been that his younger son had shown some spirit at last. Did I do it to please him? I think that is probably the explanation. Not only a conformist but moody, introvert and almost pathologically shy, I wanted to show him that I, too, was capable of reckless deeds. When, in 1982, *The Observer* published a profile of me, it was the title – 'Maverick of the old school tie' – that I wished that my father had been alive to see.

How far sibling rivalry really was responsible for an almost compulsive desire to do or say something that caught the eye, it is impossible to know. The conformist and the maverick in me existed side by side. When I became a headmaster, they complemented one another, the conformist providing a respectable base from which the maverick could make occasional forays into controversy.

Other characteristics of the child reappeared in the headmaster. When parents at Westminster said to me, 'Headmastering must be a lonely job,' it does not seem to have occurred to them that this might have been one of the chief attractions. As a child I lived in a world of my own. I do not remember being unhappy, just preoccupied with internal battles against fear of the dark and of the dentist, against nightmares, and against the hypochondria that, like an inconsiderate guest, arrived early in my life and left late. My shyness cut me off from other children. Though I set off for parties at their houses I seldom got there, preferring to turn back and leave Angus to go on alone.

My intense dislike of the first boarding-school to which I was sent at the age of nine re-enforced my inclination to turn inwards. How my father hit upon West Buckland School in North Devon I do not know; even by wartime standards it was a dump, whose only possible merit was that it was so far off the beaten track that no German aeroplane could find it. Angus and I arrived in deep midwinter when the dark stone building rose like a medieval keep out of the snowdrifts. It was a place of no escape in what, to our suburban eyes, was a bleak and wind-bent wilderness. This was not the Devon of thatched cottages and cream teas. The school was on the edge of Exmoor. Even if I had had the courage to run away, I would not have got far; the heavy rains made the moors treacherous and the few farms near the school were small and mean, offering little hope of hospitality.

West Buckland may not have been as bad as I remember it but it must have been at a low point in its fortunes. I can only assume that the headmaster, about whom I can remember nothing, either did not know or did not care what went on in the dark corridors and echoing day rooms. No disaster that befalls a school is so profound in its impact as the appointment of a weak headmaster. A small private boarding-school, out of the public eye and with no tradition to speak of, is particularly vulnerable. It soon sinks to a level that would not be tolerated in a better-known institution: buildings fall into disrepair; masters are engaged whose past is not too carefully scrutinized; power is delegated by default so that the strongest boys at every age are free to exercise a local tyranny.

I can discern in those dark days no happy moments or bright faces, though there must have been some. The one boy whose face I recall wet his bed almost every night and in the morning had to carry his reeking sheet past all the other boys in the dormitory. Angus, the fighter, battled his way through the four terms we spent there, literally battled sometimes, for I remember watching from a window as he held his own against three other boys. I withdrew into my shell, hoping to find security in anonymity.

From the horrors of West Buckland, Hitler rescued me. The invasion of Russia relieved the pressure on London sufficiently for us to be moved to a boarding school nearer home. I wish I could feel again the secret joy I must have felt (secret because it would have been tempting fortune to show it in my face or manner) as the school bus left for Barnstaple station, but memory's net catches only irrelevant flotsam; one of the few things I can remember now is the chorus of the school song. It is a cheerfully bad jingle that might have fallen from a Christmas cracker:

'Then hail to the school that by the grace of heaven
Took root and bore fruit in the hills of north Devon.'

Last year, at the age of sixty, I was invited to be the guest speaker at the annual dinner of the Old West Buckland Association. They did not know that I was a former pupil since I had suppressed all reference to my time there. It was an invitation I could not refuse, rather as a former concentration camp inmate might feel unable to resist an invitation to address the annual reunion of the Waffen-SS. When I arrived at the hotel, I looked round the crowded room to see if there was anyone I recognized. An elderly man introduced himself as a retired member of staff. I told him I had been at the school during the war. He shook his head. 'I remember an Angus Rae,' he said. 'Were you his brother?'

Despite the rivalry and jealousies that must have existed, Angus and I got on well together. I enjoyed his protection and he seemed to take a genuine pride in my early success as a sportsman. He was a talented runner and became the public schools' 800-metre champion; I was a talented swimmer, particularly over long distances. The loneliness of the long distance swimmer suited my temperament. In our approach to racing, we were predictably different. Whereas he won races from the front I would never commit myself to winning but waited until the race was nearly over before putting in a final burst that might or might not carry me to victory.

My curious tactics reflected a compromise between the uncompetitive and competitive sides of my nature, between the reluctance to commit myself and the ambition to do well particularly in my father's eyes, between the passive, introvert child and the young bully whose sudden outbursts of aggression made contemporaries wary. 'You're just a thug, Rae,' the boy cried as I sent him flying with a flurry of punches. I was thirteen and head boy of the private preparatory school to which I had been sent after West Buckland; he was a rival who, in some way I cannot recall, had defied my authority.

One Westminster housemaster was in the habit of describing any awkward adolescent as 'rather a Jekyll and Hyde character', but I told him he might as well have the phrase printed on all his report forms. The contradictory moods that can make some adolescents so difficult to live with reflect a permanent not a transient reality. As adults we bring the contradictions under control but our personalities remain coalitions whose members may have little in common other than a need to present a united front to the world.

The contradictions in my attitude to public schools also had clearly identifiable roots in childhood and youth. My father's medical career, first as a general practitioner in Taunton and then as a consultant radiologist in London, gave my brother and me provisional membership of the middle classes but we lacked some of the essential attributes of middle-class status. We had no public school connections (my father had been educated at a minor public school called Bishop's Stortford of which no one had heard), and both our parents' families were Celtic in origin and Nonconformist in religion. The English, Anglican, public school establishment meant nothing to us.

Our parents were marvellously unpretentious people whose dislike of social snobbery was passed on to their children. Angus and I and our two younger sisters, Bobby and Susan, grew up in a happy and secure home but in mid-twentieth-century England there was no escaping the anxieties caused by the clearly delineated social strata. The children who lived at the wrong end of our south London suburb were 'herps' who went to the local elementary schools; middle-class families who were more established than our own sent their sons to the better-known public schools; the rich and well-connected sent their sons to Eton and Harrow. When I told my father that I had been appointed to teach history at Harrow, he exclaimed 'Not *the* Harrow!' Even then, in the mid-1950s, a successful doctor, who had himself been to Cambridge, still regarded Harrow as a world apart.

Snobbery is not an exclusively English vice but in England from the middle of the nineteenth century it took a peculiarly English form. Your social status was defined by where you had been at school. It was not just a question of whether you had attended a public school: that merely distinguished you from the masses. What mattered was where your school fitted into the public school hierarchy. Molière would have relished the chance to depict the snubs and humiliations involved in the quintessential English game of 'trump your neighbour's school'. The value of the cards was known to everyone who played; small boys in preparatory schools could tell you that Eton trumped Harrow, that Harrow trumped Haileybury and so on. There was much talk at the time of the public schools developing character but the principal characteristic this game developed was the dreadful English disease of deference. What made the game bearable was that it was always possible to snub someone lower down the hierarchy, unless, of course, your school was at the bottom. My father's school, to which Angus and I were

sent as boarders in 1942, was as near the bottom as made no difference.

To attribute my adult ambivalence towards public schools
entirely to Bishop's Stortford's lowly position in the hierarchy
would be too simplistic. It was in my nature to be ambivalent. But
my ability to flirt with the Labour Party while applying for the
headmastership of Eton must have owed something to the contradictory emotions inspired by having to play the public school game
in my youth with poor cards in my hand.

Most of the public schools founded in the nineteenth century
aped the manners and customs of the older and more exclusive
establishments, particularly in their identification with the Church
of England. As that left the Nonconformists out in the cold, the
Congregational Church decided to found its own schools; Taunton
School in Somerset was one, Bishop's Stortford College in Hert-
fordshire was another. The principal virtue of the Nonconformist
schools was that they were unpretentious; they would offer a sound
education at a modest cost without the social trappings; the result
was that they were looked down on by other public schools whose
only claim to superiority lay in their bogus traditions and visiting
bishops.

Bishop's Stortford was a better school than its more pretentious
rivals. Angus and I were not model pupils. Angus was wild but his
lunacies were generally good-natured. When I reached adolescence,
the least I could do was give the authorities as good a run for their
money as he had done. I resigned from the cadet corps. I played
truant. I was the ringleader of an adolescent gang that picked on
the weaker masters and made their lives unbearable. Two of our
victims – Dr Plaut and Herr Berger – were refugees. Plaut had
been in a concentration camp and was almost blind. When we
reduced their lessons to chaos, the new headmaster, Arthur Evans,
appealed to our better nature, a lost cause if ever there was one.
We were not concerned with hard luck stories; if the men could
not keep order, they should not have been appointed.

In other ways, too, my adolescence followed a familiar pattern.
Sport, poetry and breaking rules were my pastimes. My ideal day
would include demanding physical activity, an hour or so in an
armchair with Swinburne or Rupert Brooke, and an escapade that

demonstrated once again my superiority over the security arrangements the school authorities had thought it necessary to put in
place. I did not regard academic work as a priority, but I had the
good fortune to encounter an inspiring teacher. Walter Strachan
taught French for Higher Certificate, the A levels of the day, but
his legacy to his pupils was a love of contemporary culture: novels,
poetry, book illustration, calligraphy, film. I lapped it up, so much
so that for a time the hooligan and the aesthete were interchange-
able roles.

Arthur Evans was a decent man but a weak headmaster. He could
be firm but his firmness lacked conviction; masters and boys who
should probably have been told to go were allowed to remain. I had
good reason to be grateful for his tolerance but the lesson was not
lost on me that a headmaster who wants to survive cannot afford
to be too forgiving. Arthur Evans was ousted by a common-room
coup shortly after I left.

In my last year at school, Evans appointed me head boy. The
transition from guerrilla leader to prime minister was easy; I
enjoyed exercising power, though the responsibilities of the job
increased my disinclination to bother with academic work. When
I failed my Higher Certificate, it was suggested that after national
service in the army I should go into industry. My father had other
ideas. He wrote to his Cambridge college and persuaded them to
let me take the scholarship examination in History. I did not win a
scholarship but I did well enough to be given a commoner place.

National service in the army confirmed my ambivalence towards
the public schools. The barrack hut to which I was assigned was
dominated by the former pupils of public schools who saw themselves as potential officers. We seldom used Christian names, preferring to call one another by the schools we had attended. I was
known as Stortford, others as Charterhouse, Stowe, Hurstpierpoint
and so on. I still think of them in that way. Charterhouse died
young. Stowe committed suicide. Hurstpierpoint became our
ambassador in Moscow.

'England isn't always going to be divided into officers and other
ranks,' says the young wife of Mr Chips in James Hilton's famous
novel. How wrong she was. However hard the state schoolboys
tried, they could never become officers. However incompetent the

public schoolboys proved to be, they seldom failed to receive the King's Commission.

There were some formalities. The Personnel Selection Officer screened the candidates before recommending those who were suitable for officer cadet training. Information from the intake ahead suggested that there was only one awkward question: 'Why do you want to be an officer?' We rehearsed various hypocrisies about leadership and service but only Charterhouse had the honesty to reply that he wanted to be an officer because that was the sort of life to which he was accustomed. It did not damage his chances.

When my turn for interview came, I was confident that the hypocrisies would see me through. But the Personnel Selection Officer opened with a different question. 'I see you were at Bishop's Stortford,' he said. 'Is that a public school?' At the end of the interview he explained that he was not turning me down for a commission, just deferring judgement. I was to go and see him again in two months. When Charterhouse, Stowe and Hurstpier-point went off to the officer cadet training unit, I was left behind, and although I became an officer soon enough, the delay and the reason for it rankled.

The four years I spent at Cambridge were the most carefree of my life. I studied History but never regarded that as the principal reason for my being there. I treated the university as a finishing school. I read widely, wrote poems and short stories, some of which were published in undergraduate journals, attended lectures unless they were too early in the morning, played games in the afternoon and devoted the evenings to the cinema or the pub. Each summer when the examinations came round, I dug out old essays and tried to memorize enough facts to drop like morsels of meat into my otherwise unappetizing answers. The examiners awarded me a degree in the second division of the second class. It was not the worst degree available but neither was it a qualification for teaching History at a good school.

I persuaded my father to let me stay at Cambridge for a fourth year to take a diploma of education. I did not know that I wanted to teach, only that I was not ready to start earning a living. It was an agreeable and undemanding year. Few people in those days took teacher training seriously and the main emphasis was on the teaching practice which I did at a Scottish public school, Fettes College in Edinburgh, whose charismatic headmaster, Donald Crichton-Miller, was to have a significant impact on my career. Meanwhile, I had met and become friendly with Daphne Simpson who was living in Cambridge. She must have thought I was an inarticulate and unromantic companion, for my idea of a good evening was to watch a cowboy film at the Regal or the Rex, but our relationship blossomed and once the bitter Cambridge spring had given way to warmer weather, we would take a bottle of wine and lie in the long grass on the river bank near Grantchester letting the summer days slip by.

Summer also brought closer the time when I would have to decide whether I wanted to be a teacher or not. I asked the university appointments board what alternatives there were for someone with my modest qualifications. 'Intelligence and security' was the answer. An ex-brigadier in a bowler hat came up from London to interview me but he was so secure I could not discover what the job entailed. It was clearly something to do with espionage but what exactly remained a mystery. As did the pay. When I asked about the salary the brigadier looked surprised as though no one had raised the subject before. I told him I would think it over.

What finally drew me into teaching was nostalgia for boyhood, not my own but the one I had experienced vicariously in the pages of the school stories that had been my staple reading until adolescence. My favourite was *The Hill*, Horace Annesley Vachell's sentimental novel about turn-of-the-century Harrow. It appealed not only to my nostalgia for boyhood but also to my longing to be accepted into the world that Vachell had created. In the public school game, Harrow was a trump card. So when the appointments board notified me that Harrow was looking for a master to teach History with a little Mathematics to the junior boys, the brigadier never had a chance. Let others guard the nation's secrets. I was going in search of an idealized boyhood on the top of Harrow Hill.

Harrow under Dr Robert Leoline James was enjoying a period of prosperity. Its beds were full and its reputation was high. Even the most famous public schools could not take their good name for granted and Harrow had experienced some sad declines under headmasters who were weak or incompetent. Fortunately for Harrow and for me, Dr James was neither. I learned the trade of schoolmastering (I say trade rather than profession because its skills, though real, are unsophisticated) from one of the best headmasters of the day. He guided me through the early difficulties of keeping order, particularly with a junior form who reckoned, not without justification, that they knew as much Mathematics as I did; and he made me feel part of the community, unlike some of the senior men who made it a rule never to speak to new members of staff until the two years' probation had been served.

When I told people I was teaching at Harrow, no one asked, 'Is that a public school?' My inferiority complex was partly cured but not my ambivalence towards public schools. Harrow also re-enforced some of my prejudices. Although I had literary pretentions, I was something of a philistine. When I became a headmaster, I did my best to encourage art, music and drama, but I did not regard them as an important part of education any more than Harrow had done.

Daphne and I decided to be married at the end of my first term. Dr James could offer us nowhere to live except a tumbledown gardener's cottage and, as he pointed out, we were lucky to get that because gardeners were more difficult to come by than historians. We decided, too, that we would like to have a family of six children. Large families were not in fashion. 'Are you Roman Catholic?' people would ask us, neatly combining religious prejudice and moral disapproval. When we produced four daughters in quick succession, one of the bachelor housemasters told his prefects over dinner that the Raes were 'breeding like rabbits' and got a good laugh. The bachelor housemaster who needed to share his misogyny with his boys was a recurring figure in our lives.

Despite the occasional misogynist, Harrow was a good place to bring up a young family. But the pay was poor; little more than one pound a day when I started in 1955. I did not think of myself as a potential headmaster and when Daphne mentioned the subject I flew into a rage. If more money was needed, I would earn it by writing. I started on a novel in the school holidays. The story, needless to say, was about boyhood. A group of London boys, evacuated to Norfolk in 1940, pursue their war games to the point of tragedy. It was an autobiographical novel on an anti-war theme and it included a romantic friendship between two thirteen-year-old boys. I thought of calling it *War Games* but, perhaps unwisely, decided on *The Custard Boys*, after 'cowardy, cowardy, custard'. The novel was published by Rupert Hart Davis and was made into a film, under the title *Reach for Glory*, by two young American producers and an English director, Philip Leacock. Though the book and the film were well reviewed they were not popular successes and my dreams of becoming a famous writer quickly faded. At Harrow, the novel and the film were seldom mentioned; it was as though I had done something which, though not technically illegal, was nevertheless faintly disreputable.

When Rupert, with a characteristic blend of kindness and good judgement, rejected my second novel, Daphne suggested that I might like to start working for a doctorate. Once again, I flew into a rage. The idea was ridiculous. But the anti-war sentiments of *The Custard Boys* had brought me into contact with a number of Quakers and I became interested in the treatment of conscientious objectors to military service in the two World Wars. I was not a pacifist but I suspected that there was a good story to be told. When I consulted Michael Howard, the Reader in War Studies at King's College, London, it appeared that the subject might be suitable for a doctorate after all, and with his encouragement, I set off on the only serious academic venture of my life.

Thus we entered on one of the happiest periods of our marriage. We had four lively and attractive young daughters. Dr James had found us a new home overlooking London on the southern slopes of Harrow Hill. I was well established as a Harrow master and increasingly interested in my research. We might well have stayed at Harrow until I retired had not economic realities tipped the scales in favour of taking risks rather than playing safe.

CHAPTER 2

A Young Man's Dream

At the start of the Autumn Term 1965, Taunton School in Somerset advertised for a headmaster and I decided to apply. I was thirty-four and had been at Harrow for eleven years. The status and benefits enjoyed by a Harrow housemaster would not come my way until I was over forty and I could not afford to wait. We had four young children and hoped to have six. Since I had no wish to condemn my family to a life of genteel poverty, I needed to earn a higher salary.

Fear of genteel poverty was reinforced by fear of failure. I dreaded reaching the age of retirement with little to show for my life but a leaving present and a round of applause at the final assembly. As a boy at Bishop's Stortford and as a young master at Harrow, I had attended these last rites often enough. There was an element of mockery in them. The audience listened to the headmaster's eulogy not so much out of respect or affection for the master who was leaving as out of fascination to see whether the headmaster, walking a tightrope between the truth and that degree of exaggeration that was considered customary on such occasions, would lose his footing. As one hyperbole followed another – 'loyal and unselfish devotion to the school', 'a fine example to us all' – the balancing act became more difficult to sustain. Meanwhile, the object of this flattery sat with his head bowed desperately trying to believe every word of it.

My determination to avoid this conclusion to my career was

strengthened by the realization that I was, as always, ambivalent. Part of me longed to stay on at Harrow and play the role of Mr Chips. If I had not married that is almost certainly what I would have done. The application for a headmastership was, therefore, a deliberate leap in the dark, a way of out-manoeuvring the passive and unadventurous side of my nature.

To pretend that in all this there was no calculated ambition would be disingenuous. I had become an Anglican at least partly because it was a requirement for most headmasterships, though not, as it happened, for Taunton. I had undertaken a doctorate at least partly to compensate for my poor degree. I had accepted an invitation to become a magistrate at least partly to encourage the selection committees to take my application seriously. For the same reason, I omitted any reference to *The Custard Boys* in my curriculum vitae in the belief that a published novel, particularly one with an anti-war theme, would not go down well with a public school governing body.

Despite the careful preparations, I was not ambitious in the same way as some of my contemporaries, who seemed to be planning each move in their career so that they would end up running one of the major public schools. I wanted to be well known but I had no plans. Nor did I have any educational philosophy. Harrow under Dr James had given me some idea what made a good school tick and how a skilful headmaster operated. I hoped it would be enough to see me through the honeymoon period; I reckoned that after that headmastering, like marriage, was something you picked up as you went along.

When I told Dr James I was thinking of applying for Taunton, he encouraged me to go ahead. I chose Taunton because the omens were good. My first patron, Donald Crichton-Miller, had started his career as a headmaster there. I had roots in the town, however shallow, and the school itself had the same Nonconformist foundation as Bishop's Stortford. With these omens, I did not bother to find out whether the school was full and financially solvent.

At the first round of interviews, I regretted this omission. Behind the imposing façade of the main school building, the classrooms and dormitories were so dark and dingy I was reminded of my miserable days at West Buckland during the war. John Leathem, who conducted me on a tour of inspection, had been headmaster for twenty years and it showed. 'All this was in a dreadful state when I arrived,' he told me. He was a classicist, an elderly bachelor who had lived with his mother in the headmaster's house until her death a few years back. He was courteous and lonely and could have been a friend; I was young and impatient and did not want his friendship. Our relationship never developed beyond the formalities that we could not avoid.

I took the first interview in my stride largely because I was no longer that interested in getting the job. When, a few days later, I received a letter inviting me to the final interview, I had to face the possibility that I might be offered the headmastership of a school at a low ebb in its fortunes. If I had had any sense, I would have realized that this was a young headmaster's dream. Instead, I considered withdrawing my application.

The situation was complicated by a recurrence of hypochondria. Shortly after the first interview at Taunton, I convinced myself that I had cancer. It was laughable, of course, a series of scenes from a Woody Allen movie, but at the time I really believed that I might be seriously ill. Daphne, ever interested in medical matters, had obtained a copy of a new booklet that listed the tell-tale signs of cancer, and I could not resist making a discreet check. My relief at discovering that I had none of the symptoms of terminal illness was short-lived. One of the signs on the list had been rectal bleeding. Within days of reading the booklet I started to pass blood. Heaven knows whether it was coincidence or an example of the mind's ability to dictate to the body.

My hypochondria was the same type of compulsive behaviour as my childhood fear of the dark. Just as I would not turn out the light until I was absolutely sure that there were no assassins in the cupboard or under the bed, so I could not get cancer out of mind until I was absolutely sure that I did not have the disease. The doctors' bland assurances seemed to leave open the possibility, however slight, that my diagnosis rather than theirs was correct. The hypochondriac clings, not to hope, but to the flimsiest reason to despair.

The date of the oral examination of my doctoral thesis was fixed for the day after the final interview at Taunton. I took both events seriously but I was also detached. The whole cancer charade may have been a subconscious device to transfer my anxiety on to an imaginary illness. In this odd frame of mind, I travelled to Taunton with Daphne for the final interview. She took one look at the headmaster's house and declared it unsuitable. I took another look at the school and regretted that I had not withdrawn after all. We stayed overnight at the Castle Hotel and decided that, if I was offered the job, I would not accept. Daphne was sick most of the night. If we had known that this time it was going to be twins we might have been less keen to reject the chance of a higher salary.

There were two other candidates on the shortlist, both older than myself and already headmasters. They were the safe candidates with a track record and they were interviewed first. When my turn came, I found myself responding to the governors' questions with all the confidence of a candidate for whom this was just a trial run. The governors were all men, mostly old boys of the school, local worthies, plus a couple of Oxford dons. They seemed a decent lot, concerned about the school's future under the recently elected Labour Government, yet open-minded about the need for change. I did not have the heart to tell them that I had doubts about accepting the job if they offered it to me.

Those familiar with such occasions will recognize at once that because I was not worried about giving the wrong answers, I had no difficulty giving the right ones. The governors were clearly impressed. Other factors were working in my favour. A number of the governors had known my father well when he had been in practice in the town. Crichton-Miller had spoken on my behalf. But there was something else that gave my candidature an edge over the competition. The great headmaster of Taunton's history had been Dr David Whittaker. For some of the men sitting round the table he was the embodiment of the school, whose long and fruitful reign had rescued it from obscurity. And Dr Whittaker, like myself, had been educated at Bishop's Stortford and Sidney Sussex College, Cambridge. That superficial coincidence was given greater significance by the fact that, to the astonishment of those who had known Dr Whittaker, my voice sounded exactly like his. Bizarre as it may seem, I feel certain that for some of the governors, these auguries were decisive. It was almost as if they believed I was the reincarnation of the great man.

The three candidates and their wives were asked to wait in an adjacent boarding-house while the governors deliberated. Conversation was difficult. The housemaster and his wife moved among us with cups of tea like relief workers at the scene of a disaster. After a while, the chairman of the governors entered and announced that I had been chosen. There were handshakes and congratulations. As the other candidates left to return to their schools, the chairman mentioned that the bursar had already given the news of my appointment to the press. Daphne and I looked at one another. Whether we liked it or not, I was going to be the next headmaster of Taunton School.

On the journey home we were accompanied in the carriage by two of the governors who had taken part in the day's proceedings. Having no wish to make conversation all the way to London, I pretended to doze off. I heard one of the governors remark on my ability to sleep at will. 'He's very lucky like that,' Daphne said, 'he can go to sleep whenever he wants to.' It was news to me but I kept my eyes closed. A rumour that I possessed unusual powers might come in handy.

The day after the interview at Taunton, I went to King's College, London, for the oral examination of my thesis. It was a relief to forget about headmasterships and concentrate on the treatment of conscientious objectors in the two World Wars. After an hour, the examiners declared themselves satisfied; they would recommend that my thesis be accepted for a PhD. I walked down the Strand and telephoned my father from a call box. When I told him about Taunton and the doctorate, he said, 'I hope that is what you want, John.' I sat in a nearby cafe and ordered a pot of tea and a chocolate eclair to celebrate. I had achieved academic respectability (it would be some time fortunately before I realized how many dull people had PhDs); with our fifth child due in the summer our family was almost complete; and the headmastership of Taunton would at least pay the bills and provide me with experience of how to do the job. In the circumstances, the thought that I might be dying of cancer seemed an irritating distraction. I went back to the call box and telephoned my doctor. I could tell from his voice that he was trying to sound surprised to hear from me. I told him that as I was taking on new responsibilities I needed to clear up this cancer business once and for all. 'Well, you'd better have an X-ray,' he said evenly. He knew perfectly well that I was a hypochondriac. The X-ray revealed that the terminal illness on which I had wasted so much time and emotion in recent weeks had been a figment of my imagination.

There is a long period of waiting between being appointed a public school headmaster and starting the job. I was appointed in December but did not take up the post until the following September. If you are moving from one headmastership to another, this can be a particularly agreeable time when you postpone the more awkward decisions on the grounds that they ought to be taken by your successor. It is a time, too, when hostilities cease. Your critics on the governing body and in the common room are so pleased to see you go, they no longer have any reason to intrigue against you. But when you are moving to a headmastership for the first time, the long wait can be frustrating.

I received a number of letters from governors and members of staff at Taunton telling me how much needed to be done. It was, they all wished to emphasize, no reflection on John Leathem who had done a wonderful job. Leathem himself was punctilious about informing me of those decisions that could not be postponed, such as the appointment of new staff. As the time for his departure drew near, he began to warn me of the difficulties he feared I might encounter. There were, he wrote on one occasion, a number of 'angry young men' on the staff – he listed them by name – who were impatient for change and who might embarrass me with demands for reform before I had had a chance to assess the situation for myself. I resented his patronizing tone and noted the names of the angry young men as potential allies.

It is as difficult for a new headmaster to be objective about his predecessor as it must be for a second husband to be objective about the first. He is sensitive, usually over-sensitive, to any suggestion that he compares unfavourably with the man he is replacing. He interprets any praise of his predecessor as a deliberate attempt to disconcert him, which it sometimes is. On the surface, relations between the outgoing and incoming headmaster are correct, even cordial; in public, they make a point of paying tribute to each other's qualities for they both have much to gain from keeping up the appearance of mutual respect. But, in private, they give vent to their true feelings which are seldom generous.

If my relations with John Leathem remained cool, my enthusiasm for the job increased with every month that passed. I began to realize that the headmastership of Taunton was not only an opportunity to revive a flagging school but also to reform those characteristics of public schools that I did not like.

As a young master at Harrow I had become secretary of a discussion group for masters under forty called the Hot Air Club. I wrote to all the members proposing that 'the Club should play a more dynamic part' in the school community and 'undertake certain definite pieces of research on aspects of school life that called for reform'. I cited school religion and compulsory games as two examples. I enjoyed the idea of being subversive but I found my colleagues less interested. They had their eye on housemasterships and did not share my enthusiasm for stirring things up.

A short while afterwards, however, the election of a Labour Government suggested a new avenue for my reforming zeal. Labour was committed to setting up a Public Schools Commission. I wrote to Reg Prentice, the Minister of State for Education, arguing that the committee should include a representative of the assistant masters in public schools and hinting – with a clumsiness that I still find embarrassing – that I was the man. Prentice invited me to go and see him. I told him – without any mandate – that the assistant masters would be sympathetic to a change in the method of entry that would undermine once and for all the public schools' social exclusiveness.

I wish I could be sure of my motivation. Opportunism certainly played a part, as did the psychological need to be on both sides at once, the honest broker between the Labour Party and the public schools. There was, too, the memory of being snubbed ('Is that a public school?') which eleven years at Harrow had not entirely erased. But I was not driven only by my hang-ups and ambition. I really did believe that there was something fundamentally wrong with a society in which education and class had such an incestuous relationship; it was almost as if the two had signed a secret pact to keep the majority of people in their place. While the public schools remained the preserve of the upper and middle classes, the state schools in which the majority of children were educated would be regarded as inferior. Thus the education system re-enforced the class system and vice versa.

I did not know how this incestuous relationship could be broken up. When I told Reg Prentice that I was in favour of changing the entry to public schools, I had no scheme in mind. I wanted schools such as Harrow to retain those characteristics I found attractive while abandoning their social exclusiveness. It was impossible, of course. Whatever those who teach in fashionable public schools may say about wishing to open their doors to all sorts and conditions of pupils, it is precisely because the schools are socially exclusive that they have developed the traditions and characteristics that make them so attractive to teach in.

Reg Prentice listened to me politely but had the good sense not to take me seriously. So I turned my mind to the problem of how to set about introducing reforms in a single school. The system could wait.

Public school headmasters have no formal training. It is assumed that if you have been an assistant master in a good school you will be able to make the transition to chief executive by virtue of the lessons you have learnt from the headmasters under whom you have served. In my case, there were only two: Donald Crichton-Miller of Fettes and Dr James of Harrow.

Their styles of headmastering were entirely different. Dr James enhanced Harrow's reputation without considering his own. He went to extraordinary lengths to keep out of the public eye. If he had any views on education, he kept them to himself. He refused to play any part in public school politics, and sat at the back during meetings of the Headmasters Conference reading *The Times*. In the school, he taught a few periods a week to the classical sixth, preached moderately well, spoke quietly and without rhetoric on public occasions and regularly entertained his masters and his senior boys to dinner. When he retired after nineteen years, the High Street of Harrow-on-the-Hill was packed with masters and boys calling for him to appear on the balcony of the headmaster's house and, when he did, they cheered him again and again as though he was a conquering hero. I doubt whether any other headmaster in modern times has had such a send-off.

The secret of his success was that he put the school before everything else. He loved his job and did not wish to spend any time away from it. He abhorred committees. From time to time, he was prevailed upon to set one up but he never took the chair himself. He had no faith in public discussion. There were only two masters' meetings a term, one at the beginning and one at the end, and he took care to arrange them so that they would be cut short by a bell summoning us to assembly in the Speech Room or service in the chapel. Masters who wished to debate issues of school policy were frustrated by the skill with which he spun out matters of little consequence.

But he always had time for individuals. Whenever I went to see him he appeared to have nothing else to do, which in a sense was true, because he had delegated the routine administration to his senior colleagues. He won our loyalty and affection by making himself available. I would enter his study determined to protest at my teaching programme or at the dilatoriness of the works department. He would wave me to chair and stand inside the fireplace sipping a cup of tea. When he had listened to my tale, he would talk about similar frustrations in his own career, how they had seemed so important at the time, how they had proved so unimportant in retrospect. By talking openly about himself as a young schoolmaster, he gave the impression that he was taking me into his confidence, and I was flattered. After half an hour or so, I emerged thinking that Harrow was the best school in the world. Years later, when members of my staff put their heads round the door and said, 'I know you are very busy, headmaster, but I wonder whether you could spare a minute,' I realized that I had my priorities wrong.

I served only one term under Donald Crichton-Miller, on the teaching practice required for my Cambridge diploma of education. I had elected to go to Fettes College in Edinburgh for no better reason than that Crichton-Miller was the uncle of the girl to whom I had addressed my adolescent, undelivered poems.

It was my first encounter with a charismatic leader. Crichton-Miller was treated by his staff and by his pupils as though he possessed superhuman powers. How far this charisma reflected the needs of his followers rather than any special quality of his own, I am not sure. The public school community of adolescents and those who choose to spend their lives educating them seems to generate a desire for inspirational leadership which is distinct from managerial competence. Perhaps that is why the idea of training headmasters has never been taken seriously and why selection committees rely so much on intuition.

At Fettes, Crichton-Miller was at the height of his powers. He dominated the school by the force of his personality. No one could doubt who was in charge. Where Dr James created the circumstances in which Harrow appeared to run itself, Crichton-Miller's presence was necessary to bring the best out in his pupils and his staff. His reputation as the strong man of the public school world made him something of a talisman for the pupils of other schools as well. When he arrived on the touchline at the start of an inter-school rugby match, the rival groups of spectators cheered and counter-cheered as though he was the president of the games and the visiting headmaster counted for nothing.

He had been appointed to his first headmastership – at Taunton School – at the age of twenty-nine. He had taken Taunton apart and put it together again in better shape. His robust methods had inspired intense loyalty. I heard him address a dinner at Taunton in the late 1960s. He singled out for praise the masters who had served him well – 'the four musketeers', he called them – and they sat gazing up at him like faithful hounds with absolute devotion.

This was the man who took me under his wing. When I started my career as a schoolmaster he was my patron and I was his protégé. Shortly after I arrived at Harrow, he left Fettes to become headmaster of Stowe. Stowe was in a bad way and the governors had appointed him as a hatchet man to get rid of the dead wood on the staff. But his methods were too ruthless for Stowe, a new school that had somehow managed to become effete without ever having been vigorous. He was opposed by a combination of governors who did not have the stomach for it and masters who feared they would be the next to go. When I heard the news of his departure, I was astounded. It was inconceivable that so powerful a headmaster could be persuaded to resign.

That was in 1963. He never got another job. When I was appointed to Taunton in 1965, he wrote to give me characteristic advice:

> The job was for me and will be for you, I hope, a young man's dream ... Achieve success in your own way and to hell with the critics. Remember also that no powerful young man wants to go in where there is no challenge. The task, as you may have gathered, is formidable, for which you will doubtless thank your Maker, as I did. I don't think you need worry about interference; anyway if you get any from Governors or Old Boys, let me know and we'll soon squash it.

His expectation that I would be a 'powerful young man' in his own image excited me and made me nervous. The aggressive side of my nature responded to his challenge but the passive side urged caution. Dr James had transformed Harrow's fortunes without spilling blood. The trouble with Dr James's approach, however, was that it took time and I was in a hurry.

In the last week of our last term at Harrow, Daphne gave birth to unidentical twin boys. We called them Shamus and Jonathan. Our joy and our family were complete. After so long with a bachelor headmaster, Taunton School was about to rediscover family life with a vengeance.

When I went to say goodbye to Dr James, he had one final piece of advice. 'Never put it on paper if you can help it,' he said. I thought he was referring to my literary efforts, which had caused him some embarrassment. When *The Custard Boys* had been published he had told me that it might have been better to have written under an assumed name. But, on this occasion, he had other compositions in mind. One of the hazards of a headmaster's life, he explained, was the provocative letters received from members of staff or parents or old boys of the school. It would be tempting to reply, answering the criticisms point by point. 'But I wouldn't if I were you,' he said. 'Ask the writers to come and see you. Talk it through face to face.' He held out his hand. 'Well, goodbye John, good luck.'

CHAPTER 3

Honeymoon

I sat alone in the headmaster's study two days before term began. The study was on the first floor, over the central entrance to the main school building, a long, grey stone edifice in the Scottish baronial style favoured by school architects in the mid-nineteenth century. The window looked out on to the school playing field where the head groundsman was putting the finishing touches to the 1st XV pitch. The study itself was small and bare. Leathem had lived frugally at school and at home. There was not even a desk, just a table with a green leather top stained with ink. When I asked the bursar to order a desk, he replied, 'I don't see why not,' as though I were asking for an optional extra. A single bookshelf in a gothic alcove held a number of hymn books, a disintegrating volume entitled *A Book of Prayers for Schools*, and an out-of-date copy of the *Public School Year Book*. In a corner cupboard was a cane hanging on a hook. I disliked the room and over the next four years spent as little time in it as possible.

But for the moment I had no choice. Tomorrow, I would face my first masters' meeting; the day after, an assembly of the whole school. What was I going to say?

The mission of a public school headmaster is to make his school more successful than its rivals. That does not preclude the pursuit of educational ideals but unless the ideals correspond to what the customer wants, the school will fail and so will the headmaster. There is nothing new about market forces in education. What made

Dr Arnold of Rugby such a successful headmaster was that his ideals accurately anticipated what the new Victorian middle classes would demand of education. He understood more clearly than any of his contemporaries that if the new money was to be attracted to the public schools, the old vices of violence and anarchy would have to be curbed. Opinions differ about Arnold's qualities as a headmaster, but there is no doubt he was an outstanding entrepreneur because he possessed the essential talent of anticipating a new trend in the market.

The public school headmaster who has no entrepreneurial instincts will not survive long. Competition is the name of the game. The style does not have to be flamboyant. Arnold was an astute publicist but Dr James filled Harrow to overflowing by trusting to word-of-mouth recommendation. Whichever approach the headmaster chooses, he is bound by strict rules, particularly on the subject of advertising. He may lie about the school's history, exaggerate the school's achievements, and massage the school's examination results but he must never say, in so many words, that his school is better than another. To the Headmasters Conference, the public school headmasters' professional association, all forms of comparative advertising are anathema. 'Eton College, a boarding-school for boys aged thirteen to eighteen' is acceptable. 'Eton College, probably the best school in the world', is not.

As a young headmaster who wished to advance his school at the expense of its rivals, I quickly learned the rules of the game (and how to bend them) and the realities of the market. It was the latter that occupied my mind on this, my first day in the office. A memorandum from the bursar drew my attention to something that John Leathem had omitted to mention: Taunton School was short of pupils.

I should not have been surprised. During the months of waiting, enough hints had been dropped in correspondence, particularly with governors, that Taunton had been allowed to slip behind the competition. The problem was boarders. There was no shortage of day boys but the school's finances depended crucially on maintaining a specific number of boarders. If Taunton was the school of last resort for those West Country boarders who could not gain entry to Sherborne, Clifton or Blundells, it was bound to be short

of boarding candidates. If, in addition, the school's reputation had
sunk so low that parents and the preparatory school headmasters
who advised them no longer considered Taunton as a boarding-
school at all we would not even pick up the rejects from the more
successful schools.

What made Taunton's position more precarious was that it had
been upstaged in recent years by one of the other public schools in
the town, a school that, in Crichton-Miller's day, Taunton had
regarded as a poor relation. There were three boys' public schools
in the town: King's College, Queen's College and Taunton School
itself. Queen's was a Methodist foundation, too small to present a
challenge to the other two. King's was the poor relation whose
fortunes had changed. Its recent history illustrated a recurring
phenomenon of the public school world: the translation of a dim
local school into a national institution by a headmaster of great
energy and few scruples. It is a variation on the theme of the headmaster as entrepreneur.

The most celebrated of these rogue headmasters (rogue because
they operated outside the conventions of the herd) was Canon
Shirley, headmaster of King's School, Canterbury from 1935 to
1966. Shirley was an egocentric, single-minded man with a flair for
public relations that almost amounted to genius. When he took
over, the King's School was so short of boys and money it appeared
to be on the point of closure; when he retired, the school's numbers
had increased from 240 to 830, its debts had been wiped out, its
buildings modernized. Shirley easily outsmarted the heads of rival
schools because they played by the rules, whereas he reduced the
ethics of headmastering to a simple proposition: whatever promoted
the reputation of King's, Canterbury was morally justified. The
Headmasters Conference kicked him out but had to re-elect him
when he became too successful to ignore.

Randall Unmack of King's College, Taunton was not quite in
the same class as Shirley but he had the same shrewd understanding
of the market in independent education. He recognized that Taunton School was King's College's immediate competitor and set
about revamping King's in the image of the old established public
schools. He played with skill on the English weakness for titles and
antiquity. He had no difficulty with titles; the West Country was

well stocked with decaying gentry whose names looked good on the notepaper. He did have a problem with antiquity; Taunton School had been founded thirty-two years earlier than King's. Undismayed, he produced a new version of history that managed to suggest that King's was a medieval foundation which had been on a par with the great schools in Tudor times. It was as brilliantly inventive as it was brazenly dishonest. And it worked. Parents who might have considered sending their sons to Taunton School were persuaded that it was King's that was a public school of long standing while Taunton, with its all-too-recent and Nonconformist origin and its day pupils wearing caps like grammar schoolboys, was not really a public school at all.

Unmack had retired the year before I went to Taunton. Of his successor I knew nothing other than that his wife was the daughter of Sir Somebody, a piece of information my secretary at Taunton had thought it necessary to give me at once, presumably to show me what I was up against.

If King's competitive edge had depended solely on small-town snobbery my task would have been easier. But Unmack's reign had coincided with John Leathem's and Leathem was an entirely uncompetitive animal. He refused to play the public-relations game according to Unmack's rules, which would not have mattered if he had ensured that Taunton was good enough to speak for itself. But he did not. He was conscientious in the routine duties of a headmaster but he seems to have regarded any innovation with distaste, perhaps because it might have been regarded as a surrender to Unmack's flamboyant style which he deplored. The more Unmack trumpeted initiatives, the more resistant to new ideas Leathem became. The more new buildings Unmack unveiled with a flourish, the more reluctant Leathem was to spend money on the fabric.

Leathem's inertia pleased the chairman of the finance committee, Horace Mole, a local accountant who regarded money spent on the school as money wasted. But it had the inevitable effect of discouraging the more enterprising members of the staff while giving comfort to those for whom schoolmastering was a refuge from more demanding employment. The Taunton School I inherited was not a bad school, but it badly needed to be shaken out of its lethargy.

That much was obvious. What was not clear to me was how to set about it. It was all very well for Crichton-Miller to say, 'Achieve success your own way and to hell with the critics.' I did not have the self-confidence that enabled men like Shirley and Unmack to go it alone. I needed allies. The angry young men who had haunted Leathem's latter days might be useful but they did not hold positions of influence. As a first-time headmaster I would have to rely, at least in the initial stages, on four people: the chairman of the governing body, the senior master, the bursar and the boy Leathem had bequeathed to me as head of school. And of these I knew that it was the senior master, Dr Ernest Neal, who held the key to my success.

On the face of it Neal and I had little in common. He was older – by ten years at least – and had spent nearly all his life, man and boy, at Taunton School. He was a zoologist whose speciality was badgers, a subject in which he had a national reputation. He and his wife Betty were staunch Nonconformists whose religious life had been touched by Moral Rearmament. They neither drank alcohol nor smoked tobacco and they regarded the cinema with suspicion.

But these differences turned out to be unimportant. At our meetings before and after my arrival, we had swiftly established a relationship of mutual respect and trust. I think he realized from the start that I was equally capable of energetic leadership and of lazy procrastination, of making unpopular decisions and of trying to avoid them; and like the good schoolmaster that he was, he played to my strengths and made me feel that I had no choice but to be the strong personality and man of principle that he wanted me to be. When I was inclined to postpone a difficult decision or a painful interview, he would say something like, 'I would do it straight away if I were you. Get it over with.'

What *I* realized from the start was that he was not going to make the decisions for me. His role was to interpret the school to the new headmaster and the new headmaster to the school. He told me what he thought I needed to know. He did not denigrate Leathem's headmastership but neither did he waste time on ritual flattery of the departed. When I sought his opinion, he gave it to me calmly and lucidly, the true scientist. But if I asked him what he thought I should do, he would smile and shake his head.

The first few weeks of term, the honeymoon period when the headmaster and his new bride are supposed to give each other the benefit of the doubt, ended abruptly when I expelled four senior boys at the beginning of November. Even before then, however, there were signs that this was not going to be a happy marriage.

The opening went smoothly enough largely because it consisted of a number of set-piece public occasions: the first masters' meeting and school assembly, the first service in chapel and old boys' dinner in the town. I may have lacked other headmasterly attributes but I knew how to hold and manipulate an audience. That does not mean that I always succeeded and I was sometimes pathetically anxious to be told that what I had said had been well received. But it was my one obvious talent for the job and it turned out to be a valuable one. A headmaster may delegate the administrative chores but he cannot delegate the task of standing up in front of the whole school and convincing the pupils and masters that he means what he says.

He should certainly not delegate the arrangements for his first encounter with the pupils. The new headmaster of a school not far from Taunton had been persuaded to submit to the following ritual. He and his wife and their two young children sat on a row of chairs behind the stage curtain in the assembly hall. When the whole school was assembled, the senior master said a few words of introduction and the curtain was raised. The sight of the headmaster and his family seated as for a photograph or perhaps for an execution, caused the school to break into peals of laughter and it was only with difficulty that the senior master regained control.

Ernest Neal had no such imaginative touches up his sleeve. My first assembly was conventional, even dull. At Westminster I enjoyed flirting with danger on public occasions, but at Taunton I concentrated on dominating the proceedings.

Demagogues are easily bored by routine administration and I was no exception. I enjoyed drafting papers outlining my plans for the development of the school but I had no idea how to construct a timetable and had no intention of finding out. It was not the logistics of running a school that excited me but the possibility of transforming it out of all recognition. I became impatient if I had to sit in my study for too long dictating letters. I wanted to be out and about making a mental note of the facilities I was going to modernize, imagining new buildings on vacant sites. I wanted to meet the boys, to talk to them informally, to get to know them, to be reassured that they did not see me as remote and unapproachable. But Taunton boys, unlike Harrovians, were not easy to engage in conversation. While I thought I was showing an interest in them, they thought I was snooping. I should have remembered that even senior boys are wary of a new headmaster. Who knows what information his casual enquiries might be designed to elicit?

My secretary, Miss Cox, did not approve of my wanderlust and filled my diary with appointments. In the first few weeks, these were mostly with members of the masters' common room. The interviews were formal and rather disjointed. I did not have Dr James's knack of putting masters at their ease. Some masters came to make sure I knew who they were and what they thought about the school. The heads of academic departments impressed upon me the importance of their subjects; the angry young men impressed upon me the importance of change (any change it appeared was better than none). Because I was anxious to have their support, I encouraged some of these men to believe that I was more sympathetic to their point of view than in reality I was.

I gave no encouragement to those who came to find out which way the wind was blowing. These were the courtiers and favourites of the former regime, men who had been too close to Leathem to be sure of their welcome. One of them had already been unwise enough to drink too much before turning up to our beginning of term party, giving the impression that he could not face the usurper unfortified.

In the third week of term, I travelled to Scotland for the annual meeting of the Headmasters Conference at St Andrew's. It was a relief to escape from Taunton; the school was too much on my mind. In the evenings, and at the weekends, I was so preoccupied with its problems that I gave little time or attention to the children. In the middle of the night, when Daphne was breast-feeding the twins, I lay on my side of the bed pretending to be asleep and rehearsing the arguments with which I would persuade the governors to spend more money on the school buildings.

At St Andrew's, the public school headmasters could forget about their penny-pinching and short-sighted governing bodies and turn their minds to the more immediate threat to their schools' existence posed by the Labour Government. The Public Schools Commission, which Labour had appointed the previous year, was clearly determined to open up the schools to the children of the working class; it was just a question of how many a school should be forced to take. Two public school headmasters sat on the Commission: John Dancy of Marlborough, who favoured opening the doors, and Tom Howarth of St Paul's, who did not.

I found the mood at St Andrew's was one of compromise and *sauve qui peut*. Most headmasters appeared to think that as reform was inevitable, they could obtain more favourable terms for themselves and their schools if they expressed enthusiasm for taking working-class children. They listened attentively to the Commission's adviser on boarding education, Dr Royston Lambert, a sociologist who had been a contemporary of mine at Sidney Sussex, Cambridge. Lambert's proposition was that as there were so many children from humble backgrounds who could be said to be in need of residential education, you could kill two birds with one stone by sending them in large numbers to fashionable boarding-schools such as Eton and Harrow. The poor children would receive a good education and the exclusive public schools would lose their social caché and be forced to adapt their middle-class values to accommodate the newcomers.

It was a preposterous piece of social engineering devised by a bachelor don who knew nothing about children and had never been to boarding-school. I am ashamed that I thought it worth considering at the time. But I was not alone. With a few exceptions such as Tom Howarth, the members of the Headmasters Conference lacked the moral and intellectual guts to attack Dr Lambert. The result was that the Public Schools Commission was re-enforced in its belief that the way to solve 'the public school problem' was to insist that half of a public school's pupils should be working-class children who needed boarding education.

I would not have been sorry to see the social pre-eminence of Eton and Harrow undermined, but not this way. I disliked the social engineers as much as I disliked the public school snobs. But I had no alternative to propose. The riddle of how to remove educational snobbery without removing the freedom to run a school independent of the state was as baffling as ever.

I travelled back to London in the company of John Carleton, the headmaster of Westminster, a charming man who was in his late fifties and within a few years of retirement. We shared a table in the dining car. He was a marvellous raconteur whose stories made light of the long journey south. Urbane and cultured, he was more like a gentleman of leisure than a headmaster. When I tried to turn the conversation on to the political and educational issues that had been debated at St Andrew's, he gently diverted me. He gave the impression that since a good education was something that a young man picked up in good company, it did not lend itself to serious discussion. As for the Labour Party's threats, he did not think they would come to anything. One of Oliver Cromwell's henchmen had demanded that Westminster School be suppressed as a hot-bed of royalism but nothing had come of that. When I told him that I was hoping to put our sons, Shamus and Jonathan, down for Westminster, he suggested that I should break my journey and have tea with him in Dean's Yard. His elegant Regency house within the Abbey precinct was a far cry from our semi-detached Victorian villa on the outskirts of Taunton. What a privilege it would be, I thought, to live in such a house in the heart of London.

Back in the provinces, I attacked Taunton's problems with renewed energy. St Andrew's and Westminster had, for different reasons, fuelled my ambition. I wanted to be somebody in the public school world. But there was no chance of that unless I could revive Taunton's fortunes. So I toured the preparatory schools of the West Country and South Wales to drum up recruits. They would come, I was sure, if I could make Taunton a more civilized place. The school's downmarket reputation was largely due to the impression that everything had been done on the cheap. A school of antiquity and prestige could get away with housing its scholars in medieval squalor. Taunton could not. There were hardly any studies for the senior boys and the school library was like a railway waiting-room in which a few bookcases had been left at random.

I told the governors that an appeal should be launched to raise funds for a new building. Horace Mole was horrified. He could not grasp the fact that Taunton operated in a competitive market and that it might, therefore, be wise to invest in improvements. On this occasion, the governing body sided with me. What – they enquired – would the appeal be for? I had already decided that the centrepiece should be a Sixth Form Centre to house a library and studying facilities.

The senior pupils said they were in favour but by the time the building started they had begun to have doubts. Wouldn't it be better to add a few studies to each of the existing houses, however architecturally grotesque such extensions would be? The house-masters were against from the start. They feared they would lose control over their senior boys if the Centre became the hub of the social as well as the academic life of the sixth form. The all-powerful housemaster, so prominent a feature of schools such as Harrow, was not part of Taunton's tradition, but I still regarded these men as over-mighty subjects who could frustrate my reforms. If the Sixth Form Centre eroded their power-base, so much the better. This was 1966. Had I known that in two years' time everybody's authority, including my own, would be under fire from rebellious pupils, I might have been less keen to weaken the housemasters' position.

The other members of the staff were reluctant to see so much money spent on a project that would address only one of Taunton's deficiencies. Conditioned by the make-do-and-mend philosophy of the past twenty years, they wanted the money raised by the appeal to be spread over a number of less glamorous projects.

I swept all these objections aside. At one of the old public schools, a new headmaster in a hurry is easily stopped in his tracks by the school establishment, but at Taunton the opposition was half-hearted and lacked a leader. Ernest Neal supported me, as did the chairman of the governing body, a mild-mannered but tough-minded Welshman called Lionel Evans. Taunton, I argued, needed the sort of facility that its competitors did not have, a showpiece that would attract parents and favourable publicity. I also wanted a striking modern building that would remind future generations of my headmastership. If the building turned out to be a folly, this delusion of grandeur would be difficult to forgive but I was confi-dent that the Sixth Form Centre was just what Taunton needed to lift it out of the doldrums.

*

One day in October I was told that senior boys were regularly cutting lessons and that masters did not bother to report them absent. When some of the boys were seen in the town, my informant explained, it confirmed local opinion that discipline at the school was as lax as it had been in Leathem's day.

I consulted Ernest Neal and the head of school, Stephen Gullick. Both thought it possible that some masters did not always report absentees but that rumours of regular or large scale absenteeism by senior boys were exaggerated. I decided that, exaggerated or not, this was an issue on which it would be important – and useful – to make a stand. I had been stung by the implication that I was as impotent as my predecessor. A little sabre-rattling would be good for my morale as well as making it clear to the masters and the boys that I would not tolerate their cavalier attitude.

I called the staff together and told them that every absentee must be reported; some of the senior men raised their eyebrows as though I was asking them to alter a time-honoured practice. Irritated by their reaction, I struck a harsher note than I had intended when I spoke to a special assembly of the school. I had meant to say that I regarded cutting lessons and leaving the school grounds as a serious offence that would be 'punished accordingly', which left my options open; instead, I managed to give the impression that the automatic punishment would be expulsion. I knew as I was speaking that I was making a mistake but the words had their own momentum and I could neither stop them nor retract them. Perhaps I was deliberately throwing down the gauntlet and daring the senior boys who sat at the back of the hall to pick it up.

If I wanted someone to defy me, I did not have to wait long. About ten days later, a junior master reported that four sixth formers had been missing from his English class. When I saw the four boys they admitted that they had been absent the whole day so that they could go to the Motor Show in London. The other masters whose lessons they had cut had not reported them absent. The boys had taken the risk because they believed that the 'time-honoured practice' would continue despite my warning. Only in the case of the junior master had they miscalculated.

I expelled the four boys and told the masters who had failed to report them absent that as far as I was concerned they were on probation. I thanked the junior master but I could not protect him from the hostility of those whose disobedience he had exposed. He resigned and left at the end of the school year. His fate re-enforced my determination to find some way of getting rid of those older masters who insisted on clinging to the attitudes of the old regime.

There were times when I was glad to see the back of a boy I had expelled but this was not one of them. The four boys had deliberately ignored a clear warning so their expulsion was not unjust but I could not help feeling that their bad miscalculation must have owed something to those members of staff who had given the impression that time-honoured practice would continue whatever the new headmaster said.

The weekend after the explusions, I walked across the playing fields to watch a school match. As I approached the touchline, the boys and masters moved away, leaving a space for me to stand alone. The honeymoon was over.

CHAPTER 4

Dictatorship

At the end of my first year as headmaster, I decided that it was time I tried once again to enter the controversy about the future of the public schools. The government's Public Schools Commission was still deliberating. There was no way in which I could influence their deliberations but I could perhaps stake a claim as a headmaster of the younger generation who recognized that the old-style public school system and its incestuous relationship with what was just beginning to be called the Establishment had had its day.

The ceremony of Commemoration which marked the close of Taunton's school year provided me with an opportunity. I wrote a speech in which I analysed the way in which the public schools had for over a century divided British society into officers and other ranks. Their powerful influence was now coming to an end. Individual independent schools would remain because Britain was a free society but for the public school *system* there was no future.

The following day, the newspapers reported the speech with the headline, 'No future for public schools.' I had known perfectly well that I was taking a risk to attract attention and the reaction was swift. Old boys of the school who were being asked to contribute to the appeal demanded to know whether I had been quoted correctly. I replied that the press had distorted the sense of what I was saying, which was true but disingenuous. Amid all the outcry, Desmond Lee, the headmaster of Winchester and chairman of the Headmasters Conference, sent me a gentle rebuke. 'There are times,' he wrote, 'when I think that the only way to avoid misrepresentation by the Press is to take a vow of silence.'

I rather enjoyed fluttering the dovecotes. It was a pleasant diversion from what Dr James had once described to me as the 'running sores' of headmastering. But, in the new school year, the 'running sores' soon reasserted themselves. From the point of view of the masters and the boys, these day-to-day problems were more important than my grand design, but I was impatient to get on with modernizing the school. Sooner or later, my autocratic methods were bound to provoke a reaction.

I was staying with the chairman of the governing body, Lionel Evans, in Cardiff, when I saw a letter lying on top of a pile of papers on his desk. It was almost as though he intended me to read it. The writer was one of those senior masters who had been close to Leathem. He wanted Lionel Evans to know how unhappy members of the staff were with the dictatorial style of the new headmaster. Changes were made without consultation; masters were being dismissed without cause. Morale in the common room was lower than at any time the writer could remember.

As a headmaster, it is better to be disliked for being decisive than for being weak. The sins of commission, even the harsh or wrong decisions, are forgiven in the end if they are thought to have contributed to the successful development of the school. But, at the time, the unpopularity hurts. Even when I was an experienced headmaster and had learnt to live with public criticism in the press and the private animosity of parents or pupils, I remained acutely sensitive to attacks on my competence by members of my staff. Such sensitivity is understandable. A headmaster can usually ride out the criticism of parents and pupils who are transient figures in the school's drama but he is very vulnerable if the staff unite against him. More public school headmasters are pushed out of office than is generally realized and in the majority of cases it is because the headmaster has lost the support of his staff. The fate of Crichton-Miller was never far from my mind.

Lionel Evans did not mention the letter to me. Its case against me was anyway overstated. Caps had disappeared to the consternation of local old boys who thought that bare heads would encourage bad behaviour on the buses; and the chapel services had been opened to wives and families to the dismay of bachelor masters who thought that the opposite sex would distract the boys from their devotions. But when it came to important changes, such as the introduction of three compulsory sciences for all boys up to O level, I had consulted all those masters, including Ernest Neal, whose judgement I trusted.

As far as the masters were concerned, the ten men who left in my first two years did so – with one exception – of their own accord, though it is true that some decided to leave while the choice was still theirs and that one resigned in protest at the policies I was pursuing. The master to whom I gave no choice was the school chaplain. He was a former congregational minister who had held the post of chaplain for twenty years. He was a conscientious and sincere man but he found it difficult to hold the attention of the boys. Though I was only a Christian fellow traveller, I had a clear idea what I wanted in a school chaplain: he must be a parish priest. The boys did not need to study the Bible or learn theology; they needed an example of Christian living.

I told the present chaplain that he would have to go; he told me that I had allowed my new-found power to go to my head. I suggested that he should return to pastoral work as a minister which he reluctantly agreed to do. I had already decided that the new chaplain should be an Anglican. This was partly snobbery: well-known public schools did not have Nonconformist chaplains. But it was also practical; I was more likely to find the man I wanted in the Church of England and denominational differences meant little to me. If St Vincent de Paul had been available I would have appointed him.

Finding a parish priest proved more difficult than I had anticipated. When I advertised, I was flooded with applications from clergymen who were trying to escape from parochial work. When I wrote to the bishops, I soon realized that the men they were recommending were those they did not want in their dioceses. Then, when I was beginning to fear that I might have to ask the present chaplain to stay on an extra term, I heard of an Old Tauntonian who was priest-in-charge of a Norman church in the new town of Hatfield. I invited him to come and see me. His name was Alec Knight. He was young, married and tough-minded and he asked a lot of awkward questions. I appointed him on the spot. It was one of the best appointments I ever made.

With so many vacancies to fill, I was able to appoint a group of young men – the new chaplain was twenty-nine, the new director of music only twenty-three – who would, I hoped, share my enthusiasm for change and act as a counterweight to the conservatism of the old guard. We set about dismantling those traditional public school compulsions – to attend chapel twice on Sundays, to watch all the first-team matches and so on – that I had tried to persuade my Harrow colleagues to question. The changes seem trivial in retrospect but they were not changes for changes' sake. I believed, as did many of the young men I had appointed, that greater freedom and choice for the pupils would make the school a livelier and happier place.

It was a mistake, though I was not the first or last headmaster to make it. Relaxing the rules does not in itself make anyone happier. What the pupils at Taunton complained about was not compulsion but boredom; they did not particularly welcome my liberalizing changes; they wanted things to do, especially over the weekend. They were suspicious of me because they were not sure of my motives. Was I making changes to establish my reputation as a reforming headmaster or because I was genuinely concerned for their welfare?

Misinterpreting their apathy, I pressed on with liberalization. Why should the boys not be trusted to produce their own magazine if they wanted to do so? Just how out of touch with their true feelings I was is suggested by the fact that I did not realize that the magazine's proposed title, *DUR*, was an acronym for 'Dictatorship Under Rae'.

Then – suddenly it seemed at the time – a wave of unrest and protest swept through the youth of almost every country in the developed world. Who or what had let the genie out of the bottle was not clear but the common denominator was an attack on adult authority in all its forms. Many of those in positions of authority, such as parents and teachers, were taken aback by the vehemence of the attack. Some lost their nerve and made one concession after another to angry offspring or militant pupils. Others, who were anxious to prevent the so-called generation gap becoming unbridgeable, tried to identify with the young, wearing their clothes and espousing their causes.

The focus of unrest was the universities but the public schools were not immune. On the contrary, the schools' attempts to regulate every aspect of their pupils' lives (when I arrived at Taunton, the rule book contained over a hundred items, one of which was 'Taps will be turned off after use'), inevitably provoked protest and disaffection. Boys refused to sing in chapel or to talk to masters until their demands were met. But there was not the open rebellion that there had been at the end of the nineteenth century in the old public schools, when Byron had planned to blow up the Harrow governors and the headmaster of Winchester had had to call in troops with bayonets to restore his authority.

The protests of the late 1960s were tame but they were still difficult to handle. I hated being at the mercy of events and not in control of them. Like so many public school headmasters of fact and fiction, I had the characteristics of an enlightened despot. If there were to be reforms, they had to be the ones I wanted and on my terms. But my position was, to say the least, ambiguous. I had already introduced some of the changes that pupils in other schools were demanding and I had weakened the authority of the housemasters on whom I would have to rely if the 'revolution' got out of hand. My position would have been stronger if I had built a closer relationship with the senior boys but I had been too busy chasing my dream of transforming the school.

The housemasters warned that further changes would be interpreted by the pupils as weakness. They thought, but did not say so to my face, that I was in difficulties of my own making. The younger masters looked to me for leadership. Did we press on with reform or call a halt until the storm of youthful unrest had passed?

My answer divided the school community. I would continue to change what I thought needed to be changed and that was all. The housemasters felt betrayed and so did the boys. The former thought I was leading the school into anarchy; the latter that I was deliberately avoiding changes that would alter the balance of power. Among the more militant pupils the right to wear different-coloured socks had been translated with alarming speed into the right to have a say in the running of the school.

At the demand for representative government, all enlightened despots reach for their revolvers. Let other public schools experiment with parliaments and elected councils; I did not intend to share power with anyone. It was not in this instance a delusion of grandeur. I believed that it would be dishonest to go through the motions of representative government when the headmaster's constitutional position meant that I would always have to make the final decision.

The winter of 1968 was a winter of discontent. The boys were surly and truculent rather than rebellious. The masters, even the younger ones, were confused about what my policy was. Reform and repression appeared to alternate with disconcerting abruptness. Meanwhile the Sixth Form Centre, which had begun to rise, was viewed not as a symbol of the new Taunton as I had hoped but as an irrelevant extravagance. I sought reassurance that I was not wholly to blame. Those I consulted were cautious; perhaps, like Macbeth's doctor, they thought it prudent not to accept my invitation to diagnose the sickness in our society.

The first half of the spring term is always the low point of the school year. In 1969, the sour mood that pervaded the school matched the wretched weather. When a young boy hanged himself in one of the boarding-houses, the tragedy seemed to some people to be all of a piece with the prevailing atmosphere of hopelessness. Whatever the reasons for the tragedy, I felt responsible. When I arrived at the scene, the doctor kneeling beside the body looked up at me and said, 'Headmaster, this boy is dead.' I walked back to our house to telephone the mother wishing with all my heart that he had said, 'Headmaster, this boy is only pretending.' Perhaps he had been only pretending and had been too young to know that make-believe can go beyond the point of no return. Would that be any consolation to the mother? I dialled the number hoping that there would be no answer. Twice as a headmaster, I had to telephone parents to tell them that their son was dead. It is the most difficult of all the duties that a headmaster is bound to undertake himself.

I asked Alec Knight to arrange a special voluntary service in the chapel the following morning. It was bitterly cold but that alone could not account for the fact that there were so few people there.

I began to lose heart but was saved from too much self-pity by my family and by the friendship of Ernest Neal and Alec Knight. I found a means of escape in writing. I had signed a contract with Oxford University Press to convert my thesis into a book and, in the evenings, I would go up to the attic in the headmaster's house and work on the manuscript.

The bitter winter also had its lighter side. The most intelligent and active advocate of reform among the boys was a member of the lower sixth called Robert Swan. We clashed over whether it was legitimate to encourage other boys not to sing in chapel. He argued that it was. I told him that if he did not wish to sing that was his business but that if he tried to organize others I would rusticate him. He ignored my warning. When I summoned him to my study to be sent home for two weeks, he pointed out that his parents were abroad at the time. 'Then you will have to stay with relatives,' I insisted. With an air of apology, he explained that there were no suitable relatives in the country either.

He had outmanoeuvred me. On the spur of the moment, I told him he would be rusticated to the headmaster's house; we had a spare room and he could live with the family. At least it would put him out of circulation for two weeks. He acknowledged defeat with good grace. The family rather enjoyed having someone to stay who was not a visiting preacher. Robert and I met at breakfast and at supper. We did not talk about the school. During the day, he worked for his history scholarship to Oxford and, in the evenings, he watched television with the children. The housemasters regarded this as further evidence of my inconsistent approach to discipline, but from every other point of view it was a satisfactory arrangement.

Spring came, but warmer weather and blue skies over the Quantock Hills did not reconcile me to the prospect of remaining at Taunton. I was approaching the end of my third year as headmaster. The received wisdom was that a young man was expected to stay for five to seven years in his first headmastership, but received wisdom was not my strong point and I determined to leave. It would be hard on the family uprooting once again but I persuaded Daphne that this time it would be for a longer stay in a better school. She had borne the brunt of my short temper and bouts of depression.

Whereas with Ernest Neal and Alec Knight, I did not reveal the true extent of my disenchantment with the job, with Daphne, I tended to exaggerate it.

Disenchantment and self-pity are two of the occupational hazards of headmastering, and I was not yet experienced enough to keep them at bay. Business schools identify 'stress tolerance', the ability to perform under pressure and in the face of opposition, as one of the key characteristics of a successful manager. At Taunton, I found that I could perform under pressure but that I allowed opposition to weaken my resolve to see my policies through to the end. By applying for other jobs so soon I was running away from the hostility I had provoked.

During the summer of 1969, two headmasterships were advertised, one at Christ's Hospital, the other at Westminster. Christ's Hospital appealed to me because its constitution meant that the pupils were admitted on the basis of need and ability, not parental wealth. The sons of the rich were specifically excluded. In such a school, I thought, I could reconcile my dislike of the officers-and-other-ranks mentality and my belief in the value of independence. So I applied and was runner-up to the successful candidate, David Newsome, a Cambridge don who had established a reputation as a historian of those Victorian headmasters who had purged the public schools of their eighteenth-century worldliness.

About Westminster, I was not so sure. Much as I liked the idea of a school in the centre of London and had enjoyed the company of the present headmaster, Westminster was one of the most prestigious public schools. It would not be easy to reconcile my contradictory attitudes there. I consulted Edward Carpenter, a canon of the Abbey and one of Westminster's governors, whom I had known for some years. He encouraged me to apply. I also consulted Dr James who struck a more cautious note. 'As far as Westminster is concerned,' he wrote, 'well, good luck to you. That is all I can say. It is not, in fact, the easiest of assignments but, of course, it is a school with a tremendous background . . . But if you go there you will be very much in the grip of tradition. Personally, that sort of thing appeals to me. I hope it does to you. If it doesn't, I do not think you will enjoy it.'

I think it was his way of saying that I was being over-ambitious.

I recognized that if I applied it would be a long shot but Westminster was a great school and I had nothing to lose.

Applying to Christ's Hospital and Westminster had the effect of dispelling my disenchantment with Taunton. My appetite for headmastering returned. I spent more time with the pupils, teaching the Oxford and Cambridge History candidates, playing water polo with the school team, debating over lunch about the right balance between freedom and discipline, arguing my case instead of just imposing it. I rediscovered what I had so much enjoyed at Harrow – the company of the senior boys.

My relations with the masters thawed too. There were still a few older men who would not be reconciled and who tried to avoid coming into contact with me, but I took to going into the common room in mid-morning break so that, after a while, even they found it difficult not to restore diplomatic relations.

None of these things made me a good headmaster or a popular one but I was learning what inexperience and insecurity had blinded me to for three years: I did not have to throw my weight about to ensure that my vision of the school's future prevailed. If I failed to be appointed to either of the headmasterships for which I had applied, perhaps I could make something of my tenure of Taunton after all.

At Christ's Hospital I did fail, though not by much. 'It may be some small consolation to you to know that you were the runner-up to the successful candidate,' the clerk to the governors wrote to me, 'and that the committee would have felt entirely happy if the decision had been in your favour.' Of Westminster, I heard nothing after the first round of interviews. Then, in the autumn, I was invited to appear before the board of governors in the Jerusalem Chamber at Westminster Abbey.

I went up early to London and called on John Carleton, who gave me a run down on the governors that was so funny I feared I would be unable to keep a straight face at the interview. Though Carleton did not say so in as many words, he made it plain that I was his favoured candidate.

I arrived at the Abbey early and hung about in the nave studying the memorials. Some Westminster boys appeared, pushing their way through the late season tourists. They were clearly using the

Abbey as a short cut to the cafés in Victoria Street. The visual contrast with Taunton boys was striking. At Taunton, the late 1960s eccentricities of appearance had had little impact, the waves of fashion becoming progressively weaker the further they travelled from the centre. Taunton boys were not given to ostentation in dress or manners, but these Westminster boys, with their flowing locks and air of sophistication, were unmistakably metropolitan.

'Dr Rae?' A large man with a military moustache and a flushed complexion had emerged, stooping through a small stone archway. 'The governing body is ready to see you now.'

The tables were arranged in a hollow square with the governors on three sides and me on the fourth. The Dean of Westminster sat opposite me, with the Dean of Christ Church, Oxford, on his right and the Master of Trinity College, Cambridge, on his left. I remember little of the interview, which lasted the best part of an hour. This time I really wanted the job but I do not think my answers to the governors' questions were any more calculated than they had been at Taunton.

Only one question sticks in the mind. Lord Butler, who had been a Conservative politician and was now Master of Trinity, asked what I would do if rebellious pupils appeared at my door demanding changes to the school rules. No doubt rebellious undergraduates at Cambridge were much in his mind. I replied that I would probably ask them in for a glass of sherry. I reckon that answer split the governing body into two camps: those who regarded me as far too liberal to be entrusted with Westminster and those who thought I had just the right political skill to steer the school through the turbulent period of youthful unrest.

After the interview, I walked across the parks to the Public Schools Club in Piccadilly. I had arranged to wait here until Edward Carpenter rang to tell me the outcome. Around half past five, I was called to the telephone. 'You will be pleased to hear,' said Edward, 'that the governors made the right decision.'

After the first round of interviews in July, the governors had chosen a short list of four. They were David Newsome, the Cambridge History don who had taught at Wellington; Alan Barker, another Cambridge History don who had taught at Eton and was now headmaster of the Leys School in Cambridge; Col Macdonald, a Classics scholar who was headmaster of Portsmouth Grammar School, and myself. But the two most powerful candidates – Newsome and Barker – had dropped out before the final interview. Newsome had been appointed headmaster of Christ's Hospital. Like myself, he had applied for both schools, but because the governors of Christ's Hospital had been quicker off the mark he had to accept their offer when it was made. Alan Barker had withdrawn because he thought he had a good chance of being appointed headmaster of Eton, a job that had unexpectedly come on the market.

The Westminster governors now faced a difficult decision. Should they go ahead with the two remaining candidates or start the whole process of selection again? Fortunately for me, they decided to go ahead. It would not look good if a school of Westminster's calibre had to re-advertise. Though I did not know it at the time, the final interview was a straight contest between Macdonald and myself.

One of the governors, Sir Henry Chisholm, refused to contemplate appointing me on the grounds that I was, in his opinion, 'a dangerous Red'. He had not forgotten the headline 'No future for public schools.' Other governors thought that, at thirty-eight, I was too young. Many years later I discovered how close the voting was. The selection committee, which had conducted the first round of interviews, unanimously recommended that Macdonald should be appointed, but their colleagues on the governing body, either because they resented having the choice made for them or because they liked me at interview, unanimously rejected the recommendation and voted for me. I was elected headmaster of Westminster by a majority of one. 'Those who were against you,' the Dean assured me when I started at Westminster, 'have now come round.' But I knew that I was going to have to work with a number of governors who had opposed my appointment.

In my final term at Taunton, Princess Anne came to open the Sixth Form Centre. It had taken three years to raise the money and complete the building. When they saw the facilities that would be available for the senior pupils, even the most sceptical critics were won over. But the real value of the project was that it raised the expectations of the school community. The paralysing spell cast by the parsimonious and parochial attitudes of the past had been broken for good. In the years following my departure, my successor, Norman Roberts, embarked on a programme of building and modernization that would have been unthinkable a few years before.

When I was at Westminster, one of the young men I had appointed at Taunton came to see me. 'The best thing you ever did for Taunton,' he told me, 'was to leave when you did.' He did not have to explain. My role at Taunton had been to shake the school out of its lethargy. I had made mistakes and enemies but when I left I took the anger and resentment away with me. Norman Roberts could move the school forward on the basis of consultation and agreement, a task which he fulfilled with conspicuous success.

I said goodbye to the school at Commemoration but their minds were on the approaching summer holidays or on the new regime to which they would have to adapt. After the ceremony in the marquee, the governors and principal guests had tea on the lawn in front of the main school building. As I was circulating, I saw one of the masters whose departure I had accelerated in my first year. He had appeared, like Banquo's ghost, in the midst of our exclusive gathering. He came up to me. 'Well, I suppose congratulations are in order,' he said. I thanked him. 'I can't say that Taunton is sorry to see you go,' he went on, 'but I hope Westminster is able to put up with you.'

CHAPTER 5

Taking Over Westminster

The roar of voices was clearly audible as I walked across Little Dean's Yard in my red cassock and black gown. I looked back briefly to where Daphne and the children were watching from the kitchen window. At the bottom of the stone steps that led up to the hall, a group of masters waited. They handed me pieces of paper on which they had written the notices they wished me to read out at this, the first gathering of the school year. Then they disappeared and I was left to mount the steps alone. Would the boys fall silent, I wondered, when I entered the back of the hall or would I have to struggle to make myself heard when I reached the dais and turned to face them? It was something I had not thought to ask.

Those masters sitting at the back of the hall stood up as I passed and the boys followed suit, row by row, in a ragged fashion. Conversation died, making way for the sound of my own footsteps. Some boys turned their heads to see what the new headmaster looked like. Others turned their heads away or looked up ostentatiously at the ceiling as though to make it clear that, as far as they were concerned, a new headmaster was a matter of complete indifference. Long hair, resting lightly on shoulders and in one case reaching half way down the back like a young girl's hair in a Victorian painting, caught my eye.

Housemasters and house tutors stood at the end of the rows. You can tell the roles that masters play in an English public school by the way they wear their gowns. Those who believe that without their steadying influence the school would lapse into chaos wear their gowns long, like ceremonial robes. Those who wish it to be known that they are on the side of the boys rather than the school establishment adopt an off-the-shoulder look. The lovable eccentric never renews his gown but lets it fade and fray until it endows him (at least in his own fantasies) with the aura of a favourite teddy bear. Westminster, I noted, had some of each.

At the front of the hall was a low dais with an ancient table whose drawer had once been used to house the headmaster's birch rods. Don't trip in this long cassock. To fall on your face at your first assembly would be a disaster from which it would be almost imposs-ible to recover; the dinner tables of London would rock with mirth as the story was told and re-told.

I placed my papers on the dark surface where boys, long dead now, had carved their names.

'Would you sit down, please.'

Immediately in front of me was a row of young scholars with short hair, new suits and innocent faces. Not for them the world-weary poses of the seventh form. It was their first term too.

How do you tell five hundred adolescent boys, most of whom regard authority as an enemy to be outwitted, that you are proud to be their headmaster? It was probably a mistake to try. I had prepared a few sentences. They had sounded rather good in rehearsal; now they sounded banal.

When I finished, a single clap threatened to precipitate an ava-lanche of ironic applause. It was one of those moments on which careers hang. I paused as long as I dared before starting on the school list, name by name, form by form, and all the time trying to disassociate my voice from the quickening of my heart. To the audience it may have appeared that the new headmaster was firmly in control but inside my cassock my shirt was soaked with per-spiration.

I had reason to be anxious. Dominating the public occasion was what I was supposed to be good at. If the first assembly went wrong, I might lose my confidence and fail to control the next. There is an element of bluff in all authority; the headmaster may be awe-inspiring in his study but at an assembly he is exposed and vulner-able. Some public school headmasters never hold assemblies while others turn their assembly halls into theatres. But Westminster's life hinged on public occasions – a daily service in the Abbey, a weekly assembly at which prayers were sung in Latin. A headmaster who could not control these occasions would soon be packing his bags. But the converse was also true. If I could establish mastery of the public occasion, my limitations as a scholar and as an administrator would matter less.

I liked Westminster from the start. During my sixteen years as headmaster, I often experienced frustration and insecurity. There were times when I was ready to throw my hand in, and times when prominent former pupils wrote to the governors demanding that I should be dismissed. On more than one occasion, I knew that I had lost the confidence of my staff. Yet, while my relations with Westminster were sometimes stormy, my liking for the school never diminished. On the contrary, the rough patches increased my sense of belonging. Whatever others thought of my suitability for the job – and there were always some who had reservations on that score – I was convinced it was the right job for me.

I arrived at Westminster with the reputation of being something of a whiz-kid which was no more deserved than the suggestion that I was 'a dangerous Red'. The whiz-kid reputation was almost entirely due to the media. My 'No future for public schools' speech had not established me as the spokesman for the younger generation of headmasters but it had put my name in the journalists' contact book. Whenever public schools were in the news, there was a chance that my opinion would be sought. I was asked to appear on radio and television programmes and to write articles for the press. It did not happen often at Taunton but it happened often enough for people who took an interest in public schools to become familiar with my name.

The impression was gained that I was one of the coming men in the public school world. I still find it odd that it is possible to build a reputation in this way and that intelligent men and women should think that because a man's opinion is sought by the press, he must be particularly good at his job. I was not deceived. I enjoyed the publicity but I knew that it had no bearing on whether or not I was a good headmaster.

I welcomed the whiz-kid reputation, nevertheless. My credentials compared unfavourably with those of my predecessors at Westminster and I needed all the help I could get. John Carleton had not been a scholar but he had spent his life at the school from the age of thirteen and his knowledge of the school's history and traditions had given him an alternative source of authority. Carleton's predecessors for four centuries had been classical scholars, in some cases of European standing. Almost all of them had been in holy orders, and graduates of either Christ Church, Oxford or Trinity College, Cambridge, the two colleges with which Henry VIII had linked the school. If their published works are now seldom read, their reputation for scholarship almost invariably earned them inclusion in the *Dictionary of National Biography*. So closely was Westminster identified with scholastic achievement that before John Carleton's appointment in 1957, it would have been unthinkable for a man without a first-class degree to be elected headmaster.

Scholastic achievement was no guarantee that a man would do the job well and I was relieved to find that one headmaster had been sent to prison for molesting boys and that others had proved inept. But the exceptions only served to emphasize the formidable tradition of scholarly headmastering that I was inheriting. If I did not measure up in the eyes of the masters and pupils, I would soon lose their respect.

In addition to scholastic achievement, Westminster headmasters were expected to possess the firmness of will without which a worldly school could not be governed. Placed as it was at the heart of the metropolis, a stone's throw from Parliament and within easy walking distance of the West End, Westminster was no ivory tower. The original William Hickey, who had been a boy at the school in the 1750s, recorded in his memoirs that he had been accosted at the school gates by thirteen-year-old prostitutes. By the late twentieth century, vice had withdrawn, but not far. There was nothing to stop a boy who had spent the morning composing Latin verses, spending the afternoon in Soho; nothing, that is, except fear of the headmaster's wrath.

This combination of scholarship and worldliness, of the pursuit of knowledge and the proximity of vice, gave the school an eighteenth-century flavour. Unlike the other great public schools, it had never been reformed in the nineteenth century and had remained impervious to the influence of Dr Arnold and his disciples. Whereas Arnold, as headmaster of Rugby, had told his senior boys, 'what we must look for is, first, religious and moral principles; secondly, gentlemanly conduct; thirdly, intellectual ability,' Westminster's tradition appeared to value these qualities in reverse order. Godliness should not take precedence over good learning. As for moral principles, the birch was a more effective means of curbing vice among clever boys than the Bible.

The prospect of being headmaster to these quick-witted adolescents in the middle of London was exciting and a little unnerving. From what I had heard and read about Westminster boys, they showed little inclination to conform. I was not sure that I possessed the firmness of will that had enabled my predecessors to impose order on this volatile mix of scholarship, worldliness and nonconformity.

John Carleton was encouraging. He was not one of those headmasters who secretly hope that their successor will compare unfavourably with themselves. He loved Westminster and he wanted me to succeed. His selflessness and his willingness to let go after nearly fifty years at the school (he had arrived as a boy at thirteen and retired as headmaster at sixty-two) was remarkable. The public school world is always buzzing with stories of headmasters and headmistresses who refuse to accept that their relationship with the school has come to an end. Some buy houses nearby and ask their successors if they can come in from time to time to take assembly; others intrigue with parents and former colleagues to engineer their successor's discomfiture or even his downfall. It is a commonplace for headmasters to haunt the scene of what they fondly imagine to have been their former glory. Geoffrey Fisher was found by his successor as headmaster of Repton sitting on the boys' beds in the dormitories, odd behaviour for a future Archbishop of Canterbury. John Leathem, too, was in the habit of returning unannounced and walking the school corridors late at night. Though all headmasters swear they will not embarrass their successor by returning too soon, it is a promise very few of them are able to keep.

John Carleton was one of the few. He never embarrassed me

though others sometimes tried to do so on his behalf. It was suggested that a new day-boy house I was proposing to create should be named 'Carleton's'. I vetoed the idea; it was nothing personal, just the necessary business of establishing the new regime. His method of briefing me was characteristic. He told me little about the formal education process; if there were problems with the curriculum or anxieties about the performance of some academic departments, he did not think them worth mentioning. Like a tribal elder, he taught me about the school by telling me stories of the past. I remember we laughed a lot together. His approach to the school's history was unsentimental. 'It is boys, after all, that make a school,' he wrote in his own book on Westminster, 'not famous Old Boys and, still less, old buildings . . . It is strange that schools should pride themselves on their antiquity when they can pride themselves on their perpetual youth.'

But while he made a point of keeping the past in its place, he did not hesitate to use it as an ally. When people complained that the boys' behaviour had never been so bad, he would observe that unlike some of their predecessors in the Seventeenth century, the boys had not yet been charged with murder. The past could be an ally, too, in teaching each new generation the spirit or ethos of the school. When the Great Hall – known simply as 'School' – was rebuilt after the Blitz, it was John Carleton who chose which former pupils should be commemorated on the walls. Alongside the coats of arms of prime ministers and archbishops, philosophers and poets, were those of popular villains and celebrated rakes, generals who had lost empires and politicians who had been executed for treason. The boys – and later the girls – who entered the hall week by week for Latin Prayers could hardly fail to learn that Westminster's former pupils had been brilliant, original, unscrupulous, treacherous and idiosyncratic but seldom dull.

Dr James had warned me that if I went to Westminster, I would be 'very much in the grip of tradition'. That was true but not, I think, in the sense he meant it. Westminster's traditions were more colourful than oppressive. The school appeared to be almost entirely free from the sillier public school conventions – of which there were plenty at Harrow – but rich in eccentric ceremony. Over the latter, the headmaster was expected to preside wearing a long red cassock which was the outward sign of his membership of the collegiate body of the Abbey and the school. When Henry VIII expelled the monks, he established Abbey and school as a joint foundation with the Dean and chapter as the school's governing body. The constitution was changed in the mid-nineteenth century, but the Dean was still chairman of the governors and the headmaster was still a member of the collegiate body with his own stall in the Abbey marked, 'Archidedasculus'. When I became headmaster, the Dean was Dr Eric Abbott, a cultured bachelor with impeccable taste and an unreliable heart. 'I may not be here when you arrive,' he told Daphne and me when we went to stay with him in the Deanery. He made a point of warning all his guests that his expectation of life was short thereby, perhaps, postponing the final heart attack for several years. I got on well enough with him though we were never close. My real friend in the cloisters was the Archdeacon, Edward Carpenter. Edward and I had met while I was teaching at Harrow and had formed a friendship that was to play an important part in my career. He acted as a referee when I applied for the headmastership of Taunton and I am sure it was he who swayed the Westminster governing body in my favour. Unlike Eric Abbott, who was a confidant of the royal family and could easily have passed for a prince of the church, Edward Carpenter was a humble, humorous man with a philosophic turn of mind and a lively interest in all sorts of ideas and people. There was a chance that he would be appointed Dean if Eric Abbott died in office, as he had so often threatened to do, but that chance was reckoned to have disappeared with the arrival of a Conservative Government in 1970. Edward was not a political priest but he made no secret of his left-of-centre sympathies.

It was Edward who put John Carleton's headmastership into perspective for me. As under master, the number two in the Westminster hierarchy, John Carleton had played the key role in rebuilding, one might almost say 'recreating', Westminster after the war. Evacuation and German incendiary bombs had damaged the school's identity and fabric to such an extent that some people doubted whether Westminster would ever recover. John Christie, who had held the school together during evacuation, was a tired man. His successor as headmaster, Walter Hamilton, was more interested in making his way in public school politics. So it was left to John Carleton, the under master, to oversee the restoration not only of the buildings but also of the ethos that gave Westminster its distinctive flavour. When he became headmaster, John Carleton completed the work of restoration.

By 1970, Westminster had re-established itself as one of the leading schools in England. Its reputation for scholarship and for tolerance of individuality, as well as its unusual provision for weekly boarding, appealed to middle-class London parents who were disenchanted with the idea of sending their sons to boarding-schools in the country, which seemed to be increasingly out of touch with contemporary life.

No headmaster anxious to be a success wishes to take over a school that is on the crest of a wave. I was relieved to hear, therefore, that Westminster still had its problems. The features that made the school attractive to some parents deterred others. Westminster had some fine buildings and an incomparable site but it was short of space and its sporting facilities were scattered around London. Well-motivated scholars flourished in its stimulating intellectual atmosphere, but boys who needed to be pushed frequently failed to fulfil their potential. Openness to the world meant that Westminster was free from some of the tensions of a country boarding-school but in the late 1960s the world offered temptations more dangerous than those that had awaited William Hickey at the school gates.

To the so-called permissive society, Westminster was peculiarly vulnerable. John Carleton's response had been characteristic: Westminster boys had for centuries been required to cope with the temptations of London so there was no cause for alarm. If John Carleton's response was too sophisticated, that of some of the governors was naive and simplistic. The governor who gave me lunch at the Athenaeum seemed to think that all the problems of the Swinging Sixties would go away if I insisted that the boys' long hair was cut. In all but one of the conversations I had before moving to Westminster – with John Carleton, with the Dean and other governors, with senior members of the staff – no one ever mentioned the word 'drugs'. The exception was an interview with Stephen Poliakoff, the boy who was editor of the *Elizabethan*, the school magazine. To his question 'What about drugs?', I replied, 'This is something you come into the school and find out about. I have no preconceived ideas.'

There was something reassuringly old-fashioned about the lamp-lighter who appeared at dusk, pushing a bicycle with a short ladder tied to the crossbar, to make the round of the gas lamps in the Abbey precincts. He belonged to the era in which my favourite school stories were set, an age of innocence when playing bridge, not smoking cannabis, was the vice for which boys could be expelled. I saw him first one September evening shortly after we had moved in, and I last saw him the day before we moved out sixteen years later. Though I often watched him set his ladder against the lamp outside the headmaster's house, climb the half-dozen rungs and open the glass case to light the gas, I never discovered why he came on some days and not on others, nor did we ever exchange a word. He would look up sometimes and, seeing that I was standing at my study window, would nod his head in an almost imperceptible gesture of recognition and I would similarly respond, as though there was some long-established secret between us. Given the number of ghosts who were supposed to haunt the precincts, I would not have been surprised to learn that he was one too.

We had a week to settle in to our new home before term started. Though Daphne and I had worried about bringing up six children in the heart of the metropolis, the Abbey precincts turned out to be a safer environment than the country town we had left. The Abbey and the school shared the site of the medieval monastery and their crowded complex of buildings and courtyards, cloisters and gardens, provided an ideal playground for young children. Shamus and Jonathan, who were just four, could disappear without causing alarm because the worst that could happen was that they would be lost in the maze. On one occasion in those early days, they were found asleep behind one of the tombs in the Abbey.

The headmaster's house was a splendid Regency building with nine bedrooms, two fine reception rooms on the first floor and a roof garden with a panoramic view of the Abbey and the Houses of Parliament. The front of the house faced Dean's Yard, the main courtyard of the precincts; the back faced Little Dean's Yard, the heart of the school, its piazza, its crossroads and its stage.

Like almost every other building in the precincts, the headmaster's house had a powerful historical charge. The house had once been occupied by F. W. Farrar, whose sentimental public school novel, *Eric or Little by Little*, had been written in what was now the headmaster's study. In Farrar's time, the house had been one of the political and literary salons of London, playing host to Gladstone, Tennyson, Ruskin, Browning and Matthew Arnold, but I was more interested in a silk banner bearing the coat of arms of Oliver Cromwell that hung in a frame outside my study door. It had lain on Cromwell's coffin as it was carried into the Abbey in 1658. A sixteen-year-old Westminster scholar called Robert Uvedale had darted from the crowd, snatched the banner, and disappeared into the crowd again before he could be caught. In later life, Uvedale became a grammar school headmaster.

The house had its disadvantages. The masters' common room was on the ground floor so that the family had to share a front door with seventy full- and part-time staff. The inner doors were seldom shut because boys and masters needed to have access to my study and my secretary's office on the first floor. For much of the day, the house was open to anyone who cared to drift in. At first, I accepted this lack of privacy as one of Westminster's eccentricities and I was slow to recognize how much the family resented the daily invasion of their home.

Most of the teaching staff lived in school property within the precincts or close by. Despite its reputation for scholarship, Westminster could not compete for the best staff unless it could offer accommodation. Nor could it continue to maintain the distinctive features of an urban residential community, in which the boarders rather than the day boys set the rhythm and style of everyday life, unless a large number of masters lived within easy reach.

In the days before term began, I met a number of the masters and noticed at once how different their attitude to me was from that of their counterparts at Taunton. With the exception of Ernest Neal and Alec Knight, none of the Taunton masters was at ease when I was around or called me by my Christian name when we were off duty. At one of the staff parties, Daphne left her handbag behind and, on returning to the room, heard one of the senior men call out, 'It's all right. We can relax now. They've gone.'

At Taunton, it was always 'Yes, headmaster', which was fine on formal occasions but, after a while, I began to wish that a few others would decide that they did not always have to stand on ceremony. For their formality, I only had myself to blame. I did not lower my guard with them and should not have been surprised that they treated me as too dangerous to approach without due deference.

The Westminster masters were friendly and polite but not deferential. They had the easy confidence of men who knew they were teaching in one of the best schools. I had the impression that they looked upon the headmaster as the first among equals; the title was always written as two words at Westminster as though to emphasize the point. I had to prove myself to men who thought that, if they put their mind to it, they could do the job just as well themselves. In some cases it was not wishful thinking. Westminster produced headmasters: the under master, Martin Rogers, was about to be appointed headmaster of Malvern College and his predecessor as under master had been appointed headmaster of Rugby. Compared with Taunton, this was a common room of high calibre.

I do not think I spent much time analysing the strengths and weaknesses of my position, at least not during the day. There was too much to get on with. But at two o'clock in the morning, the case against me could seem overwhelming. I had failed A levels; I had a poor degree; I came from an unknown public school and an undistinguished college; I had never been a housemaster or head of an academic department and my experience as headmaster had been a mere four years in a school almost as low in the hierarchy as my own. Westminster boys and Westminster masters would soon call my bluff. As for the governors, on whom my continuing in the job depended, half of them had been opposed to my appointment in the first place.

The case for the defence was not altogether convincing but it was enough to take the sting out of my anxieties and allow me to drift off to sleep again. My doctorate did not compensate for my poor academic qualifications but it helped to screen them. It would help, too, that the part of my thesis that dealt with the First World War would be published two weeks after term began under the title

Conscience and Politics. Similarly, the Harrow connection helped to divert attention from my unfashionable education. I could do nothing immediately about the doubts in the minds of governors, but I hoped they would disappear if I could quickly establish my authority as headmaster.

The headmaster of an English public school exercises considerable power and patronage but that does not guarantee him the respect of the pupils and the masters. He may strut upon the stage and make his bondsmen tremble but he can only establish his authority by the quality of his performance and the strength of his personality. From the very first day, the school watches to see how well he handles the public occasions, how determined he is to impose his will, what interest he shows in different aspects of school life and how calmly he resolves the numerous conflicts and crises that occur in a community.

This combination of power and vulnerability, of being an absolute monarch yet permanently on trial, suited me well. I was lazy and easily bored. I needed a job in which there was risk as well as opportunity, in which I would stand or fall by my own efforts. At Taunton, I had seldom thought about the risk of falling. I was in too much of a hurry. But I could not take Westminster by storm. Martin Rogers had made it clear to me that, while some things at Westminster needed changing, I should consult the masters and not rush in with reforms of my own. One of the older housemasters, who had evidently taken my whiz-kid reputation seriously, made a similar point. 'Westminster does not need to be knocked about,' he advised me, 'it only needs a little fine tuning.'

The trouble was that knocking schools about was the limit of my experience. I did not know how to fine tune a school and I had been careful to avoid consulting the masters too often at Taunton. I arrived at Westminster believing that a headmaster was judged not so much by the skill with which he managed the everyday life of the school but by the speed and determination with which he tackled its problems.

A boy in his second year at Westminster was required to act as a 'substance' to one of the new boys – his 'shadow'. The substance ensured that his shadow was in the right place at the right time, that he understood what was left of Westminster's argot and that he kept out of trouble. For a new headmaster, two people performed the role of substance; the captain of the school and the under master.

The captain of the school, a post once held by such disparate figures as Charles Wesley and Warren Hastings, was David Drew, a mature young man who took his Oxford entrance exams, his role as head boy, his captaincy of the football XI and his wet-nursing of the new headmaster in his stride. He could have made his way in politics or in business but his ambition was to be an archaeologist, an ambition that after Oxford he fulfilled.

It is often said that to be the head pupil of a school is an excellent preparation for leadership, but it is politics not leadership that the young man learns, the arts of manipulating people and situations, of defusing crises and deflecting danger, above all of reconciling conflicting interests. The head of school stands at the point where adult authority and youthful rebellion meet. He has to satisfy the headmaster that he can be trusted to enforce the law while satisfying his contemporaries that he is not in the headmaster's pocket.

Like most Westminster boys of his age, David Drew was sophisticated in his handling of adults. He must have realized that beneath the confident exterior I sometimes wavered in my resolve. As Ernest Neal had done at Taunton, this seventeen-year-old helped to strengthen my determination when I was tempted to postpone an unpopular decision. 'If you back off now,' he told me firmly on one occasion, 'you will lose respect.'

The under master at Westminster was both deputy headmaster and housemaster of the Queen's Scholars. Whereas most public schools distributed their scholars round the houses, Westminster, like Eton and Winchester, housed them all in one building known as College. In previous centuries, the under master had been a man whose seniority and experience gave him authority among his peers in the masters' common room. When he had urged support for the headmaster he had been listened to. But, in more recent times, the under mastership had been given to a young man who was expected to move on after a few years to become a headmaster in his own right.

Martin Rogers was a friend and Cambridge contemporary but I

would not have the advantage of working with him for long. When his appointment as headmaster of Malvern was confirmed, I was faced with the problem of choosing a successor when I had little knowledge of the personalities involved. Though Martin advised me, the choice had to be mine. The man I chose would be my closest ally during the period when I was trying to establish my authority at Westminster.

There appeared to be three candidates, all of whom were in their late twenties or early thirties. Two of them were gifted bachelor teachers who, in relation to the pupils they taught, gave and received intense loyalty. The third was a married man, a no less gifted teacher but one whose emotional life was centred on the family. Both the bachelors had their supporters among the senior members of the common room but I chose the married man. I reckoned that he was more likely to be able to stand apart from the cliques and intrigues that occur in any academic community and I was convinced that he would be a better housemaster of College. The forty scholars, selected by a fiercely competitive exam and set apart from the rest of the school, formed an élite within an élite. The last thing they needed was a housemaster whose emotional life centred on them.

Jim Cogan remained my under master for fifteen years. Though, from time to time, I suggested he should apply for a head-mastership, he was not interested. He enjoyed teaching too much and had no ambition to have a command of his own. What I came to like most about him and what others found unsettling, was that he judged every question on its merits. He was able to detach himself from his personal likes and dislikes and apply his powers of reasoning to the issue in hand. His detachment was easily misinter-preted; governors on the executive committee, whose meetings Jim attended, thought him intellectually arrogant and unprincipled, but he was neither. It is true that he lacked political nous – his willing-ness to see both sides of an argument could be exasperating when other members of a committee had clearly indicated that as far as they were concerned the discussion was at an end – but he more than made up for this by the moral courage with which he was prepared to pursue an unpopular line both with governing body and with the common room.

From my point of view, Jim Cogan's political limitations were a small price to pay for having an under master who was loyal and whose assessment of his pupils and colleagues was not distorted by the cross-currents of clique and emotion. He saw things and people in their true perspective. When other housemasters, particularly towards the end of a long term, over-reacted to a schoolboy peccadilo he argued for keeping a sense of proportion. I have only once known him disconcerted by the eccentricities of adolescent behaviour and that was when he discovered that one of his scholars was keeping a young boa constrictor in his study as a pet. (John Carleton would no doubt have commented that, in the early nineteenth century, scholars were in the habit of keeping fighting cocks under the floorboards in the dormitory.)

When I announced Jim's appointment as under master, one of the bachelor candidates handed in his resignation. In his letter, he said he was exhausted and that his pupils, 'who have shown a touching concern for my welfare', had suggested that he needed a rest. I talked him out of it because his departure would have reflected badly on me, but he became one of my sharpest critics and did not hesitate to share his low opinion of me with like-minded colleagues. At the time, I did not know how critical he was, which was just as well; if a headmaster knew what people were saying about him behind his back he would never sleep at night.

Among the pupils, hostility to the new regime was unfocussed and episodic. Though a headmaster needs the respect of the pupils and can be in serious trouble if respect is lost or withheld, the pupils themselves are not as interested in the headmaster as he thinks they are. They have their own lives to get on with. The headmaster is a remote figure with whom most have little direct contact. Ask any former public schoolboy what he thought of his headmaster and he will most probably say, 'I hardly ever saw him.'

But, as I had discovered at Taunton, a new headmaster who tries to change things is viewed with suspicion. Even Westminster's sophisticated and supposedly radical pupils liked things the way they were. My first attempt at change met with little resistance, however. It is difficult now to recall the strength of feeling that could be aroused twenty years ago by the length of a schoolboy's hair. Many adults regarded long hair as a challenge to their authority; many teenagers regarded the right to wear their hair the way they pleased as the touchstone of liberty. John Carleton had, as usual, taken the historical line. I admired his refusal to fuss over fashion but I knew perfectly well that I could not follow his example. If I did nothing, it would be assumed that I was as 'liberal' as my detractors on the governing body had feared.

I disliked the label 'liberal' – another consequence of my speech casting doubts on the future of public schools – but it clung to me, nevertheless. 'His attitudes seemed to be generally (or typically) liberal,' Stephen Poliakoff had written in the *Elizabethan* at the time of my appointment but he had mistaken evasive answers for liberal ones. My instincts were autocratic not liberal. Towards the public schools as a whole I would always be ambivalent but in the school of which I was headmaster any relaxation of the rules would be on my terms. At Taunton, I had been in favour of greater freedom for the boys because their lives were so hedged about with silly restrictions; pulling these restrictions down had been my way of making an impact on the school. But, at Westminster, the boys already enjoyed so much freedom compared with their contemporaries in country boarding-schools, that a policy of further liberalization would be as unwise as it was unnecessary.

How I was going to make an impact on Westminster, I did not know. My immediate concern was survival. Those who have not done the job are surprised to learn that public school headmasters worry about being sacked. It doesn't show. But even when I was well established at Westminster, I feared that I might be given notice to quit. In my first term, I treated every problem as a test of my fitness for the task. I told the boys they would have to get their hair cut because I knew that this was the trial of strength the school had been anticipating. The issue was trivial enough but – as David Drew warned – to have backed off would have meant losing respect.

After making the announcement at Latin Prayers, I watched anxiously over the following days to see whether it had had any effect. If some of the long-haired boys defied me, I did not know what I should do; for a new headmaster of Westminster to send boys home for not getting their hair cut would be to risk exposing his authority to ridicule. I was relieved, therefore, when, with much grumbling and procrastination, the cavalier locks were cut. The *Elizabethan* commented: 'Hardly had the first few weeks passed before West-minster's characteristic long hair had, with surprisingly little pro-test, vanished.'

In one of my favourite Western films, US cavalrymen easily defeat a group of Red Indians and, riding in pursuit of their foe, suddenly find themselves confronted by a vast army of warriors. The ease with which the long-haired boys were brought into line was similarly deceptive. Behind that superficial evidence of West-minster's *laissez faire* approach to discipline lay a more formidable problem.

I knew little about the nature and use of illegal drugs. I assumed that the smoking of cannabis – a drug I had never seen – was confined to fringe groups and that the majority of teenagers, par-ticularly those in public schools, were not affected. At Taunton, the question of illegal drugs had never arisen. At Westminster, the school rules banned the use of tobacco and set strict limits to the boys' access to alcohol, but illegal drugs were not mentioned. Apart from the boy editor of the *Elizabethan*, no one had thought to raise the subject with me. Yet the use of cannabis was so widespread at Westminster that the drug was sold openly in Little Dean's Yard and across the tables in College Hall. I can only assume that the masters knew and had decided to turn a blind eye, or that they did not know, in which case they were dangerously out of touch.

Just how widespread the use of cannabis was is suggested by the comments of the senior boys who were interviewed by the press when the story broke in the *Sunday Telegraph*.

'I have taken drugs often and I could easily get hold of some in school if I wanted,' one seventeen-year-old was reported as saying. 'You have to have experience of taking cannabis to understand why we take it. It is harmless and stimulating and lots of boys take the drug regularly and do not see it as a menace.' Another sixth former was more explicit: 'I have worked out that half of the senior boys in the upper school take or have tried cannabis. There is nothing wrong in smoking pot but, if you think there is, then a situation exists at Westminster which you would consider serious. We get hold of the stuff both inside and out of the school. Some days boys bring it in and some get it at parties at weekends. But I could get you some immediately if I wanted to.'

To these statements, the journalist added a damning observation: 'It must be emphasized that both boys were intelligent and well-spoken. They dressed smartly and did not brag about drug-taking. They seemed to regard it as a usual practice rather than an adventure.'

My own enquiries revealed the almost routine nature of drug abuse. When I asked the school monitors, they were understandably cautious; while it was true that some senior boys 'had experimented with cannabis', mostly at weekend parties, few would risk bringing the stuff into the school. But, as I pointed out to them, there had up to now been no risk because the school authorities had chosen to do nothing.

Once I became aware of what was going on, which was halfway through my first term, doing nothing was no longer an option. But the very extent of the problem made it difficult to know how to deal with it. Over a hundred boys could be involved; I could not expel or rusticate them all, though I was tempted to threaten to do so, if only to shake the masters and governors out of their complacency. What made me angry was not the behaviour of the boys but the cowardice of the adults. As far as I could see, most of the masters and governors had not wanted to know the truth; it had been so much easier to persuade themselves that if there was a problem, it could safely be left to the new headmaster to solve. But it is no use a headmaster cursing the past; he is paid to deal with the problems he finds, not to apportion blame. However much he may enjoy formulating a devastating critique of the former regime in his imagination, in reality he alone will be held responsible if the problems are not confronted.

I considered warning the school that from now on anyone involved with illegal drugs would be expelled, but I did not believe that the warning would be taken seriously, unless I had demonstrated that I really meant what I said. Any expulsion would risk attracting the attention of the press and if journalists discovered that half the sixth form were taking drugs, Westminster's reputation could be badly damaged. But I was prepared to take the risk because I feared that the truth would come out anyway and thought it better that the story should be 'Headmaster tackles drug problem' than 'Public school sixth form riddled with drugs'.

It was one thing to decide on a tough policy but quite another to find the evidence against a particular individual. I could not pick on a few boys at random as though I were a First World War general dealing with a mutinous regiment. The chances of masters making an arrest, or of the school monitors turning in one of their contemporaries, seemed to be small. There was nothing for it but to wait.

I was wrong about the monitors. Shortly after half term they reported that a fifteen-year-old boy had been distributing cannabis in College Hall at tea time. I questioned the boy. He did not deny it. He seemed rather surprised that I should be interested. I expelled him. There were echoes of my first term at Taunton. The school authorities had, by their apparent indifference, given the impression that they did not rate drug abuse very high in the calendar of crimes. But I thought the expulsion was justified both by the facts of the case and by the need to deter others. The boy's housemaster put up no fight and I rather suspected that he was not altogether sorry to see the boy go. The boy's parents lived overseas. His uncle came to see me. He asked whether there was any chance of my changing my mind. I said that there was not. He said that was what he had expected.

Almost immediately, other cases came to light. I expelled one more boy and rusticated four others. There I was determined to stop. I called a special assembly, explained why the boys had been punished and warned that possession of illegal drugs would result in rustication, while those who brought drugs into the school for sale or distribution would be expelled. Later, I would realize that this distinction between possession and sale was a false one but, at the time, it seemed the best way of limiting the damage that would be caused by a large number of expulsions.

The damage was considerable nevertheless. The press put the story on the front page. When journalists telephoned, I said: 'I have no evidence that cannabis is readily available in the school' but the boys they interviewed told a different story. In the competitive world of independent schools, Westminster's rivals would be rubbing their hands together. How many prospective parents were likely to be put off by 'Westminster's drug problem' it was impossible to tell; I could only hope that by taking a firm line I had conveyed the impression that the problem was being brought under control.

Dr James wrote to me from Harrow: 'You certainly chose the right time to make a real drive at the drug problem, which I think most people knew before you ever went there was a considerable problem at that particular school in that particular situation.' But many of the senior boys at Westminster thought I had overreacted. The *Elizabethan* which, unlike most school magazines, was free to comment on such matters, reported: 'Towards the end of term there was a fuss about drugs, a problem which was admitted to be widespread. The expulsion and rustication of several boys aroused general indignation.'

My first term at Westminster ended as it had begun with a public occasion at which my authority seemed to hang in the balance. On the last day the pupils competed for prizes at 'Orations', a long-established custom consisting of the declamation of prose and verse (preferably in Latin or Greek or by a well-known Westminster author or politician) before the whole school. The headmaster sat at the back of the hall.

I felt relaxed. The end of term was only a few hours away. As I listened to the young scholars spouting Latin as though it was their native tongue, I looked forward to the days of unwinding when the boys had gone and to the pleasures of our first family Christmas in the Abbey precincts. Tomorrow, we would go together to Covent Garden to buy the Christmas tree.

A seventh former stepped on to the stage to announce his subject. '"King John's Christmas",' he proclaimed, 'by A. A. Milne.' A ripple of mirth ran through his audience which became open laughter as the poem proceeded.

> King John was not a good man –
> He had his little ways.
> And sometimes no one spoke to him
> For days and days and days.
> And men who came across him,
> When walking in the town,
> Gave him a supercilious stare,

> Or passed with noses in the air –
> And *bad* King John stood dumbly there,
> Blushing beneath his crown.

If that was the extent of their indignation, I could afford to join in the applause.

The orations were judged and the prizes distributed. I walked to the front of the hall. The school monitors joined me on the stage like a praetorian guard. David Drew's expression said, 'Keep it short'.

'Taking over a school such as Westminster,' I began, determined, despite the uncertain temper of the audience, to break the golden rule that headmasters should never try to be funny, 'can be a hair-raising business.' For a second, the school was silent, as though trying to make up its mind whether it was with the new headmaster or against him. The modest laughter that followed left the question unanswered.

I wished them all a good holiday and a happy Christmas. The masters hurried to the exit with the boys crowding behind them. I watched them go, glad to have survived the term, my authority neither established beyond doubt nor damaged beyond repair.

CHAPTER 6

The Competitive Edge

For me, the most enjoyable aspect of headmastering was the relations with pupils; the most difficult was the relations with staff; the most frustrating, the relations with governors. But my dominant preoccupation for sixteen years was how to make Westminster a more successful school than its rivals. I had no fantasies about being a great headmaster. My first thought was of survival. But, as I grew in confidence, anxiety about surviving there, though seldom absent for long, took second place to my desire to sharpen Westminster's competitive edge.

Westminster's reputation as a leading school was less securely based than appeared at first sight. Its academic record depended too much on the success of a handful of pupils. Its unconventional style oscillated dangerously between respect for non-conformity and easy acceptance of hedonism. Its fine buildings would have provided comfortable accommodation for three hundred pupils but, by 1970, they housed almost five hundred.

There was, therefore, an element of illusion, even deception, in the image that Westminster projected to prospective parents. The school's virtues were real but its no less real limitations were hidden. Westminster publicized its success in getting pupils into Oxford or Cambridge colleges but did not publish its public examination results, which would have revealed how many boys ended up with poor A levels or no A levels at all. Much play was made of the unique advantage of being in the centre of London – the museums, the theatres, the art galleries – but parents who imagined their son on a five-star introduction to Western culture discovered too late that he spent most of his spare time wandering aimlessly round the Army & Navy Stores.

These limitations were quickly apparent. Less immediately obvious – neither the governors nor the masters appear to have realized what was happening – was the effect of the changing balance of boarders and day-boys. The number of boarders was falling while the demand for day places grew stronger every year. The total number in the school could be maintained without difficulty but every time a boarder was replaced by a day-boy the fee income went down, while the cost of running the school remained the same. Unless the number of day-boys increased faster than the fall in boarders, the school would be operating at a loss. In other words, the school would have to expand to make ends meet. The catch was that there was nowhere to expand.

My attempts to solve these problems were less decisive and systematic than they appear in retrospect. I could not railroad the governors and masters as I had done at Taunton. I had to learn the art of institutional politics: how to persuade, manipulate, intrigue and outmanoeuvre. The autocrat in me chafed at the slowness of it all. I had to submit to governors' recommendations when I did not think that they were qualified to judge the issues involved; I felt obliged to set up committees of masters to consider questions to which I already knew the answer. Why could they not see that Westminster had to change if it was to compete successfully with its rivals? If more and more boarders went to country boarding-schools, if potential scholars chose Eton or Winchester, if too many bright day-boys chose St Paul's, then Westminster was in trouble. It was as simple as that, and it alternately maddened and depressed me that some members of the governing body and the common room refused to recognize that Westminster was operating in a competitive market.

Fortunately, many of the younger masters grasped the economic realities as firmly as I did. And I had allies among the governors. Edward Carpenter remained a good friend and loyal supporter throughout my headmastership, though there were times when I must have tested his loyalty to breaking point. In 1974, he was appointed Dean by Harold Wilson and thus became, *ex officio*, chairman of Westminster's governing body.

The support of Lord Trend was almost as important to me. Burke Trend joined the governing body in my first term when he was still secretary to the cabinet and swiftly became its most influential member. He did not assert himself but his advice was almost invariably followed. The source of his authority was not so much his personal prestige, or his mastery of the way committees work, as his wise judgement. He knew so much about men and affairs, you felt that any course of action he proposed could not be improved upon. I was fascinated to see how he applied the skills he had developed at the centre of power to the parochial problems of the school. I turned to him often for help and he never let me down.

Neither Edward Carpenter nor Burke Trend approved of all the strategies I employed to make Westminster more competitive, but without their support I do not think I would have survived so long.

The rivalry with other schools appealed to my fighting instinct. Towards the end of my headmastership I invited Michael Brearley, the former England cricket captain, to do some part-time teaching at Westminster. One of the unexpected benefits was that I could engage Michael in discussions on the psychology of leadership. On one occasion, he took me to task for seeing the headmaster's role so much in terms of confrontation, of battles to be won and enemies to be defeated. In relation to the rivalry between schools, he was right: I did see it as a battle that Westminster had to win.

The quality of the opposition varied. In the competition for scholars, Eton and Winchester had great advantages. Whereas Westminster had no endowment, they could draw on their considerable wealth to subsidize fees and provide a range of facilities that put Westminster's to shame. But while Eton always had the edge over Westminster, Winchester did not. In Michael McCrum and Eric Anderson, Eton had had two outstanding headmasters. Michael McCrum transformed Eton's academic standards (to the rage of Old Etonians he insisted that entry to the school should be solely by competitive exam) and he persuaded the housemasters to abolish the last trappings of the old-style public school, such as fagging. He made Eton a powerhouse of efficient organization. Under his leadership and that of Eric Anderson his successor, Eton was not just the best-known but the best-run independent school in the country.

Winchester never presented a comparable challenge. Despite its wealth, its antiquity and its reputation for scholarship, it was not the outstanding school it should have been. It produced good academic results and not much else. Introspective and rather self-satisfied, it needed a headmaster who would shake the place from top to bottom; luckily for Westminster, the Fellows of Winchester fought shy of appointing that sort of man.

The competition for scholars was limited to these two schools; the competition for boarders could come from any of the major boarding-schools. Here again, Westminster was in luck. Radley was the only boarding-school, apart from Eton, that greatly enhanced its reputation in this period, thanks to the leadership of Dennis Silk, the most widely-respected headmaster of his generation.

The competition for day-boys focussed on to one school – St Paul's. It had a succession of good headmasters – Tom Howarth and Warwick Hele in my time – its academic standards were higher than Westminster's and, despite being in London, it managed to avoid the whiff of decadence that hung about Westminster's reputation. It had two other points in its favour: its fees were lower than Westminster's and it was more welcoming to boys from London's large Jewish community.

I decided that the way to make Westminster more successful than its rivals was to achieve such high academic standards for all the pupils that the school's other and more intractable limitations would matter less. The talent was there, I was convinced. But Westminster wasted much of it by treating its pupils as though they were university undergraduates who could safely be left to motivate themselves. The masters who favoured this approach saw themselves as university tutors rather than mere schoolteachers, hence their reluctance to take responsibility for matters of school discipline such as drugs.

There was something admirable about the way the cleverest boys were allowed to pursue their own intellectual interests and to treat the examination syllabus with the contempt that it no doubt deserved. This was the way Westminster's most gifted pupils had been educated for centuries. Christopher Wren had hardly bothered to attend formal classes and since Robert Hooke had mastered the first six books of Euclid in one week there was not a great deal left for him to learn even from his formidable headmaster, Dr Busby. But you cannot base a system of education on the eccentric demands of genius. The speed of a runaway horse, as Jean Cocteau observed, does not count. Even if Westminster had more runaway horses than most schools, this did not justify denying the majority of pupils the academic structure they needed.

The protagonists of the existing arrangements insisted that the cleverer boys should pass through the lower school as quickly as possible in order to spend the maximum time on their specialist studies. These boys took O level within a year or so of arriving at Westminster (in some cases they had taken some O levels at their preparatory school at the age of thirteen). They were thus required to choose their specialist subjects at fourteen or fifteen, to take A level at sixteen or seventeen and to spend a further year or more preparing for their Oxford or Cambridge scholarships. It was this final year, the seventh form, that was regarded by many masters and boys as the glory of a Westminster education.

I set out to destroy the seventh form. It absorbed the time and energy of the best teachers. It diminished the importance of A-level grades which were, for most boys, the passport to higher education. It forced the more able to specialize long before they were in a position to know what it was they wanted to specialize in, with the result that many chose Latin and Greek, the subjects at which they had excelled at their preparatory school. They did not know whether they would have preferred science because most preparatory schools at the time treated science as a peripheral subject. Above all, the emphasis on the seventh form meant that many boys who were not scholars failed to achieve their potential.

One reform was sufficient. If all boys had to spend at least two years in the lower school, the seventh form would wither away. The runaway horses would champ at the bit but the majority would benefit.

The defenders of the seventh form fought hard, none more so than the head of Classics, Theo Zinn. Theo was a man of wide human sympathies and considerable charm. He was also a tenacious politician. When I thought I had outmanoeuvred him, he returned to the fray with fresh arguments which he proposed in such a reasonable manner I almost fell into the trap of thinking he had modified his position. I liked him but I was not taken in. What he really feared was that if he did not catch his future classicists young, they would be attracted to other subjects. The seventh form was first and foremost a device for maintaining the privileged position of Classics at Westminster.

The boys in the classical seventh sprang to Theo's defence in the pages of the *Elizabethan*. His allies in the common room accused me of being a barbarian and a philistine, of wanting to turn Westminster into an exam factory and of sacrificing 'true' education to the demands of the market. But most of the masters needed little persuasion; though they may have regretted the passing of the seventh form, they recognized that Westminster could not compete with other schools if it continued to allow a minority to dictate the academic priorities.

This change set Westminster on course to become one of the handful of consistently successful academic schools. It had always been known for producing scholars; now, with any luck, it would catch up with its rivals in bringing the best out in all its pupils. No sooner had this change been made than the academic standard was threatened from another quarter. The fall in boarders and the rise in inflation of the early 1970s forced me to expand the total numbers. Quite apart from the problem of where to put them, there was a danger that we would have to lower the entry standard. Though the demand for day-boy places was strong, that did not mean that all the candidates were of the right academic quality. On the contrary, the pool of talent on which Westminster was drawing was restricted, not least by the day fees, which were the highest in the country.

High fees were not the only problem. Westminster, like Winchester, had its own entrance exam. This gave Westminster a certain cachet but, in inflationary times, fewer and fewer preparatory schools could afford to run a special form for Westminster candidates. There was no doubt that Westminster was losing good boys to rival schools who used the Common Entrance Exam. Once again, the old guard argued that something intrinsic to Westminster was at stake; once again, I insisted that Westminster would have to change.

Another deterrent to prospective parents was Westminster's reputation for anti-Semitism, a reputation that was not undeserved. I set out to change it, not because I was particularly enlightened, but because I did not see why St Paul's should be allowed to corner the market in bright Jewish boys. The reputation was of recent origin. In the 1960s, it had been made a condition of entry to College as a Queen's Scholar that the candidate 'professed the Christian faith'. There was nothing in the school's statutes to justify such conditions and the suspicion was that it had been introduced to bar the increasing number of Jewish boys who wanted to compete for scholarships at Westminster. At the same time, the number of Jewish town boys or non-scholars admitted to the school was strictly limited by the registrar who controlled Westminster's entry. The registrar in the 1960s was a former Indian Army colonel. It must be said in the colonel's favour that he was not a hypocrite; when Jewish parents applied, he made it clear that they were not welcome. Though some Jewish boys were admitted, the Jewish community had no doubt about Westminster's attitude.

The more I looked into this question, the less I liked it. I read the notes that the colonel made of his interviews with Jewish parents. His comments formed a consistent pattern:

Both parents came to make the registration. They brought the little boy with them. They were vulgar and unattractive.

Personally, I thought the father was conceited and obnoxious. In fact, I took a violent dislike to him. I am sure he is very wealthy.

She seemed a very nice person, anxious to do her best for the boy. She was, however, very common and I do not think we want the boy.

Mother came to make the registration (mother-of-pearl finger nails); I did not care for her.

The mother came to make the registration (jaguar and chauffeur) nice clothes but the bangles! Very common speech and talked through her nose.

I thought her an unattractive parent; ugly voice and really Jewish in appearance.

I do not know why Walter Hamilton had let the colonel loose on Westminster's entry or how much he or John Carleton knew about the policy that the colonel was pursuing. What a mockery it made of Westminster's claim that unlike the more conventional public schools it was interested in talent rather than background.

The colonel had retired before I arrived but the deterrent effect of his policy was as strong as ever. It seemed to me that the quickest way to give a signal that the policy had changed would be to remove the condition that barred Jewish boys from winning Queen's Scholarships. I put up a paper to the governing body proposing this. I had only been at Westminster two years and I did not know how the governors would react. I assumed that after some discussion, the majority would side with me. What I had not bargained for was the strength of their desire to protect the Anglican tradition; the school had long-standing links with the Abbey and with the monarch who was the head of the Church. It was the scholars of Westminster School who greeted the new sovereign at the coronation service with cries of '*Vivat!*'

The English establishment, to which most of the governors undoubtedly belonged, is nothing if not pragmatic. When my paper on Jewish scholars was debated, I made the mistake of arguing that it was a matter of principle that the Queen's Scholarships should be open to any boy regardless of his faith. Sir Henry Chisholm (he who had labelled me a 'dangerous Red') declared that he would resign rather than agree to the fundamental change I was proposing. But when I changed tack and argued that we needed all the bright boys we could get if we were to become a leading academic school, the opposition crumbled. Chisholm had second thoughts; if the change was being made on purely pragmatic grounds, he did not think it would be necessary to resign. With no further discussion, the requirement that a Queen's Scholar must 'profess the Christian faith' was swept away.

As guardians of the Anglican tradition, the Westminster governors were more wary of Roman Catholics than of Jews. There was no barrier to the admission of Roman Catholic boys but suspicion of Roman Catholicism was a recurring theme at governing body meetings. When I proposed that a new house should be named after John Dryden, one of Westminster's most famous poets, it was opposed on the grounds that Dryden had been a Roman Catholic. When the Lord Chancellor wrote to propose the removal of the ban on a Roman Catholic becoming headmaster of Eton, Winchester or Westminster, a ban that dated back to the Test Act of 1673, Eton and Winchester agreed without a second thought, but Westminster's governors did so only grudgingly. Heaven knows what they thought when Daphne became a Roman Catholic in 1976.

Despite knowing how touchy they were on this subject, I put to them a request I had received from the Cardinal in connection with the Pope's visit to Britain. For reasons of security, it had been suggested that the Pope should travel by helicopter from Gatwick airport to central London and that the school's playing field at Vincent Square would be a convenient landing place close to the Catholic cathedral. I mentioned the request casually under 'any other business' and was delighted to hear these intelligent men engage in a serious discussion on whether the head of the Roman Catholic Church could be allowed to set foot on the Protestant playing field. Some appealed to the school's statutes; others to the school's history. Even Burke Trend had misgivings. 'He doesn't even recognize our orders,' he reminded me. It was as though they believed that if Westminster School was to accommodate the Pope, however fleetingly, all that had been achieved in the long struggle to establish the Protestant succession would be put at risk.

In the event, the Pope decided to travel by train, which was just as well. There were far fewer objections when I proposed that girls should be admitted to Westminster's sixth form. Girls, like Jews, were not a threat to Protestantism. When I arrived in 1970, a handful of girls from Francis Holland School were attending A-level classes in science. Their position was anomalous. They were not Westminster pupils, just visitors. I thought it would make more sense for them to become full members of the school and for the same status to be offered to other girls who wanted to study in Westminster's sixth form. There was no opposition from the common room and so I put a formal proposal to the governors in 1972.

It is tempting, looking back, to assume that I must have had a well-thought-out motive. But I did not. It just seemed the logical step. John Dancy had introduced girls to Marlborough's sixth form in 1969, so I was not breaking new ground. Like Dancy, I probably saw the girls as agents for change, though I doubt whether I was clear exactly what change I had in mind. Marlborough was a large country boarding-school to which the girls had come like pioneer ladies bringing the first trappings of civilization to a frontier town. But Westminster did not need civilizing; if anything it was too civilized. There was something precious and artificial about a community in which there were so many boys whose intellectual growth had outrun their physical and emotional maturity. Perhaps it was this artificiality that I hoped the girls would help me to dispel.

Whatever I imagined would happen, the principal benefit of opening the sixth form to girls was to increase the pool of academic talent on which Westminster was able to draw. It was the admission of girls more than any other factor that enabled Westminster to raise its overall academic standard at the same time as increasing the numbers in the school. In 1970, there were 480 pupils; when I left in 1986, there were 630. Without the increase, Westminster would have been in serious financial difficulty; without the girls, its academic standard would have fallen behind that of its competitors.

Westminster's high academic standard did not, as I had hoped, distract the attention of prospective parents from the lack of space or the spectre of drugs.

Trying to solve the first of these problems was like digging a hole in fine sand; every time I created more space on the monastic site, it was filled by the increasing numbers in the school. I would like to have bought a building nearby but the governors would not hear of it. Westminster's finances were a mystery to me, and the chairman of the executive committee, Sir Henry Chisholm, did his best to see that they remained so. He was an accountant by training and had spent most of his life in industry. Despite the fact that we disagreed about almost everything, we got on rather well. But I found his secretiveness about the school's finances infuriating. He clearly believed that the less the headmaster knew about the money available the better.

It took me some years to discover the true picture. Though Westminster had no endowment and no City livery company to act as fairy godmother, it was not exactly impoverished. It had accumulated capital over the years. It also had access to the resources that former pupils had contributed to the Westminster School Society, set up before the Second World War by an old Westminster who had been barred from the governing body because he was a Roman Catholic. These two funds could probably have provided the school with a total of three quarters of a million pounds, though even that sum would not go far in the property market around Westminster. Nor would it put Westminster on a par with its competitors. During the same period in the early 1970s, Eton had an income of a million pounds *a year* from its investments.

One of the former pupils to whom Westminster had reason to be grateful was A. A. Milne. He left the school a quarter of his royalties and that sum – about £40,000 a year – was also allowed to accumulate. By the early 1980s, Westminster could at last contemplate buying property to accommodate the expansion of the 1970s. In 1981, the school bought a former hospital in Vincent Square which became an enlarged preparatory school (increasing once again the pool of talent) and in 1986, the year that I left, an office block in Smith Square, which was converted into a Science Department and opened in 1987.

In the meantime, we made do, like any other inner city school, by using the same space for a variety of activities. We would never have the new libraries and swimming pools, the specialist teaching blocks and extensive playing fields of our competitors, but we had in Mr Drummond, our clerk of works, a scene-changer of great ingenuity who could transform a classroom into a fencing salon and a fencing salon into a theatre in the course of an afternoon. It was galling to look over the wall and see the spacious accommodation occupied by the Abbey clergy whose minimal responsibilities hardly justified their being housed there at all. But anyone who has lived cheek by jowl with a dean and chapter knows that, whatever the

Church of England may lack in spiritual insight and moral leadership, it more than makes up for in the jealousy with which it guards its property. There was no chance of the school expanding into the empty spaces around the cloisters.

Much more damaging than lack of space was Westminster's reputation as a 'druggy' school. We asked parents who had registered their son and then decided to send him to another school to complete an anonymous questionnaire. To the question 'Why did you decide *not* to send your son to Westminster?', the answer that appeared most frequently was along the lines of 'Drugs, permissiveness etc.' This, more than anything else, blunted Westminster's competitive edge and gave its rivals an easy advantage.

In this case, I did have a clear idea from the start what I wanted to achieve. My aim was to get rid of Westminster's reputation for permissiveness, particularly on the question of drugs, while retaining its repuation for being more mature than the country boarding-schools in its handling of the wild oats of adolescence. If I could strike the right balance between giving Westminster pupils too much freedom and imposing too many restrictions, I might be able to turn Westminster's vulnerability to advantage. Many boarding-schools treated adolescents as though they were children. Might not a Westminster education, stripped of its too-permissive attitude, be a better preparation for life at university and beyond?

Needless to say, it was a difficult policy to pursue and I do not know whether or not I was successful. Some masters and pupils thought that I had turned a civilized school into a police state. Interviewed by the *Tatler* in 1984, a boy who had been at Westminster in the 1970s passed this judgement: 'During my time there the entire attitude changed under Dr Rae. He got rid of the old-fashioned, sleazy, drunk teachers and replaced them with henchmen – ambitious, unpleasant men. Drugs were his bogey. He'd terrorize boys to find out where it was going on.'

The use of illegal drugs was not the only or the most common disciplinary problem that public school headmasters had to face but it was the most difficult to get to grips with, let alone solve. In the Westminster context, it illustrates better than any of the more familiar vices how hard it was to steer a course between the permissive society and the police state.

There was an important difference between the use of illegal drugs and the more familiar schoolboy vices: in the case of drugs, the pupils knew more about the subject than the school authorities. Headmasters spoke about the dangers of cannabis, using the slang – pot, dope, grass – in an attempt to establish their credentials, but they had never seen the drug and had only the haziest notions about its effect. Drugs were seldom discussed at private meetings of the Headmasters Conference and it was unthinkable that they should appear on the agenda of the public Annual General Meeting. Drugs were bad news, like mad cow disease. Headmasters wanted to reassure the customers that isolated outbreaks did not amount to an epidemic.

From a commercial point of view, this made sense, but it inhibited open debate and the development of an agreed policy which would have helped both headmasters and parents. It also encouraged some headmasters to turn a deaf ear to rumours of drugs in their schools. It paid to do nothing. If no boys were punished, there was no risk of reports in the press from which parents would conclude that the school had a drug problem.

It also paid to point the finger – not too directly – at another school. Headmasters of country boarding-schools, when quizzed by parents, were in the habit of saying, 'We do not have a drug problem but we're certainly not complacent. We're just thankful that the school is not in the centre of London.'

Country boarding-schools *did* have a drug problem but because they were more cut off from the source of supply the problem surfaced less frequently and tended to be confined to a small group of pupils. Westminster was not cut off from the source of supply. Boys could buy cannabis casually in Piccadilly or Leicester Square, or establish a regular trade with contacts they made at parties and in pubs. As almost all the boarders went home at the weekends, both boarders and day boys had easy access to London's drug culture. Many parents did not know what was going on. Of those who did, some said nothing, while others condoned their son's use of illegal drugs. Some parents smoked cannabis themselves.

After the experience of drugs in my first term, I wanted to earn the reputation for taking a hard line. Drugs were indeed my 'bogey' in the sense that I regarded them as the most serious threat to

Westminster's survival as a leading school. That did not mean that I conducted witch hunts. A headmaster who is over-zealous in his determination to expose his pupils' crimes will soon find that he has few pupils left. On the other hand, I had to be seen to follow up any rumour of drugs because only by doing so could I convince the pupils that I really did intend to keep drugs out of the school. For the time being, I did not concern myself with what happened away from the school at weekends and in the holidays.

A drugs case always started with a rumour. No boy was ever caught smoking a 'joint' in his study, though one imaginative boy grew cannabis plants in his window box, which his unsuspecting housemaster commented on favourably. The most likely source of a rumour was a parent or a senior pupil. Some parents made anonymous telephone calls, others came to see me and gave me information on the condition that I never revealed where it had come from. Most senior pupils, including school monitors, did not regard it as their job to pass on information about their contemporaries but they were prepared to alert their housemasters if they thought that younger boys in the house were starting to use drugs.

Rumours of drugs were never brought to me by the self-appointed guardians of discipline in the common room. These men were only too eager to tell me that pupils were flouting other school rules or making a mockery of the uniform regulations, but they kept well away from the drug problem. 'We must have a blitz on smoking, headmaster,' or 'boys' manners,' or 'punctuality', but no one ever suggested a blitz on drugs. It was not that the teaching staff were in favour of legalizing cannabis (though some of them may have been), but they knew so little about the drug culture that they did not wish to commit themselves. The governing body were similarly reluctant. On more than one occasion, they had long discussions about the scruffy appearance of the boys and girls and gave me detailed advice on those areas of disarray that needed to be checked, but on the question of whether pupils should be expelled for using illegal drugs they preferred not to express an opinion.

I can plot, from the pages of the journal I kept from 1973 onwards, the frequency with which the drug rumours occurred. It was approximately once a term. Those who have worked in schools will not be surprised to learn that they were most likely to occur in

November and February, the two low points of the school year. An entry in my journal for 1984 illustrates the form in which the rumour might arrive:

A parent rings. Rummaging in her son's room, she has found a letter from a girl and read it. [This sort of detective work in children's bedrooms is a characteristic of mothers rather than fathers. Mothers want to know too much; fathers don't want to know enough.] The letter urges the boy to keep away from drugs and reveals that X is selling drugs in the school. Now X, aged sixteen, is one of the brightest and best of the sixth form, talented academically and musically, and with literary gifts. What must I do? Anxiety about the resurgence of the drug problem is already on my mind as publicity has been given to the increase in heroin and cocaine use in the UK. I shall see X and his parents – the sooner the better.

X denied having anything to do with drugs and his parents were outraged that he should have been accused. I let the matter drop. I could not question the girl or the boy to whom the letter had been written because I had undertaken not to do so. No doubt if X had not been one of the 'brightest and best', I would have followed up this rumour with greater determination. But there are times when a headmaster does not want to know the truth. There were other occasions when my pursuit of a rumour that came to me alone was inhibited by the thought that it came too soon after the last one; the school did not need another expulsion to re-enforce the deterrent and I was loath to give my critics on the staff an excuse to claim that my policy was a failure. But these were the exceptions. In most cases, the rumour had to be pursued to the very end, and that meant interrogating the pupils who were under suspicion. For centuries, public school headmasters had bullied and blackmailed their pupils to get at the truth. The advent of illegal drugs gave a fresh twist to this well-established practice because everything depended on obtaining a confession. I did not 'terrorize' the pupils to make them confess but there were times when I was so anxious to crack a case that I knew I had reached the frontier that divides the headmaster from the secret policeman.

The headmaster's dilemma is a familiar one. A boy is suspected of selling drugs in the school but he denies doing so and no one is prepared to give evidence against him. If the headmaster takes no further action he may be putting more boys at risk and will certainly give confusing signals about his own attitude. Since I left Westminster, a number of former pupils have told me that they were amazed that I did nothing about boys whose involvement in drugs was well known to everyone. The answer I give to them is that I did not have the evidence.

How far would it have been morally right to go in order to extract the truth? Some headmasters asked the local police to conduct the interrogation for them; others, in more recent years, have insisted that a boy suspected of using drugs should be sent to the school doctor for a urine test. I thought that the best way to protect the pupils and the school's reputation was to make it a high risk for boys or girls to use drugs. Instead of bringing in outsiders to increase the chances of detection, I raised the stakes. Whereas I had started by distinguishing between the 'pusher' and the 'user', within a few years I decided that any involvement in drugs would result in automatic expulsion. I also extended the application of the rule so that it covered what happened away from the school at weekends and in the holidays.

The more draconian the rule, the fewer the drug rumours that surfaced. I had the impression, as did prospective parents, that Westminster was a less druggy school. It is probably true that fewer pupils risked bringing drugs into the school but I have no evidence that my policy altered one way or the other the amount of drug-taking in holidays and at the weekends. My attempts to introduce drug education were spasmodic and I fear they had little impact. The doctors, psychiatrists, policemen and reformed addicts I invited to talk to the pupils seemed incapable of striking the right note. In particular, they were very reluctant to pass judgement. But the longer I stayed at Westminster, the more I saw the drug problem in terms of weakness of character. In this I was at odds with contemporary views on health education which emphasized the health risks and rejected any suggestion that people who were slaves to drugs lacked moral fibre.

I do not think I was wrong. Whether or not to surrender your freedom of choice to a drug is a moral issue as well as a health issue.

I wish now that when I spoke to the new boys about drugs, I had placed as much emphasis on the moral implications as I did on the legal and medical facts. That I did not do so was because I regarded illegal drugs as the most serious threat both to individual pupils and to Westminster's reputation. I wanted quick results. The keenness of the competition between schools favoured deterrence rather than the slow-burning fuse of moral education. The two are not mutually exclusive but when prospective parents ask about 'drugs, permissiveness etc.', it is tempting to settle for the former.

Despite all these strategies to make Westminster more successful than its rivals, I still felt the need to publicize the school at every opportunity. It is difficult for me, now, to disentangle my own desire to be in the public eye from my more calculated attempts to manipulate Westminster's reputation. Perhaps the two were, in practice, inseparable. Most critics thought that I was more interested in publicizing myself than the school.

As far as Westminster was concerned, even those who disliked my promiscuous relationship with the media, acknowledged that it did the school no harm. 'His notorious PR operation in Westminster,' one of them wrote after I had left, 'culminating in an unctuous television documentary calculated to lift the profile several miles, paid off superbly.' As I have already pointed out, public school headmasters are of necessity entrepreneurs. Whether they like it or not, they are concerned with the outside world's perception of the school. They do not, unless they are stupid, mistake the image for the reality; all the public relations in the world will not convince parents that a bad school is a good one. But the right sort of publicity can give one good school the edge over another and it was this that I was seeking.

What attracted parents to Westminster was the academic standard and the Westminster style, an intangible quality that was variously but inadequately described as 'civilized', 'tolerant' and 'liberal'. What put parents off were factors that I could never change: London would always be on the doorstep and the school would always be short of space. The ideal publicity, therefore, would draw attention to Westminster's good qualities while drawing a veil over its limitations.

There were risks. Journalists and television producers could not be bullied and blackmailed. But I thought the rewards of successful publicity were worth the gamble. What distinguished me from most of my colleagues in the Headmasters' Conference was not that they did not want good publicity for their schools but that I was more willing to take the risks.

The BBC's documentary film on Westminster was made in 1979. When the producer, Eddie Mirzoeff, and the director, Jonathan Gili, made a tentative approach, I knew at once that I wanted the film to be made. The danger of bad publicity, of a boy saying to camera, 'Everybody here smokes dope,' only made the prospect more exciting. It was not so much publicity that I could not resist, as the hint of danger. But my assessment of the risks and rewards was level-headed enough. I knew that everything depended on whether I could trust Mirzoeff and Gili. As it happened, Mirzoeff had three sons at St Paul's and sending a St Paul's parent to film Westminster was rather like sending a Campbell to make a documentary about the Macdonalds of Glencoe. A more substantial doubt crossed my mind when Mirzoeff said that his aim was 'to dispel some myths about public schools'. I did not doubt his sincerity but I knew, even if he did not, that some of the so-called myths had a firm basis in truth. Mirzoeff might discover that the public schools had not 'changed out of all recognition' as some of their apologists claimed.

Any doubts I had, I suppressed. I trusted Mirzoeff and Gili. They insisted on retaining editorial control; I was confident that Westminster's good qualities would dictate the tenor of the film. But my confidence was not shared by every member of the common room and the governing body. The masters who expressed misgivings, such as Theo Zinn, the head of classics, were probably in a minority but I did not put it to the vote. I told the governing body that, with a few dissenting voices, the common room was in favour of the film being made. A majority of governors were in favour, too, but only on the condition that they retained editorial control. I pointed out that this was not on offer; Mirzoeff and Gili were making a television film not a commercial for Westminster. With the help of Burke Trend, the master craftsman of resolutions that would not be hostages to fortune, I steered them towards a vague compromise. 'What does that resolution mean?' asked an Oxford philosopher who had doubts about the film. 'It does not mean anything,' the Dean replied. 'What would it mean if it did mean something?' the philosopher persisted. 'I think,' said the Dean, 'we may safely leave the interpretation to the headmaster.'

Never before had film cameras been given unconditional access to a public school. Gili let the cameras roll for a few days without telling the pupils or the masters that there was no film in them. When the novelty had worn off, he started to film in earnest. With great patience, and an unusual gift for being unobtrusive, he and his team shot twenty-one hours of film which would be reduced to a sixty-five-minute documentary. For the most part, he concentrated on the lives and opinions of the pupils but towards the end he filmed a meeting of housemasters and heads of department to discuss changes in the academic curriculum. It was dull stuff and I was surprised that he thought it worthwhile. But halfway through the meeting, Theo Zinn, who had been so opposed to the whole project, launched into a deeply-felt and eloquent defence of Westminster's classics. I could not interrupt him without looking clumsy. It was a brilliant performance which exploited the occasion and medium in a way that made the rest of us seem amateur and it was the only part of the meeting that remained in the final film. What a mistake it is to underestimate the cunning of unworldly academics.

The film was shown on BBC1 at the beginning of the new school year in September. I was delighted with it. Gili had captured the urbane, idiosyncratic world of Westminster without falling completely under its spell. Questions were asked about drugs but the boys and girls managed to give the impression that the headmaster's hard line had driven the problem out of the school. The only embarrassing moment occurred by accident. A girl was filmed consulting her housemaster about university entrance but, because his study was small and it was difficult to get both girl and housemaster into the same shot, she was asked to sit on the edge of his desk. The result was a scene that provoked a number of angry letters, one complaining of the girl's 'damnably bad manners'.

The reaction of the press the next day was so favourable as to be almost disconcerting. According to the *Daily Telegraph*, the film was the best PR for the public schools since the battle of Waterloo.

Television critics dwelt on the beautiful surroundings, the excellent teaching and on 'the articulacy and endearing frankness' of the pupils. The general view seemed to be that the sooner all schools in England were like Westminster the better.

Such sentiments were not calculated to win Westminster new friends or to appease those the film had offended. Many supporters of the public schools were irritated by the 'cocky selfconfidence' of the boys and girls. This was not the sort of public school they had known and had expected to see: no prefects, no hierarchical deference, no lines of boys cheering their heroes from the stricken field. 'My son, my late husband, and many of my friends and their sons went to public schools,' wrote one correspondent, 'and I can assure you that none of them were as portrayed on your programme.'

Opponents of the public schools were equally incensed at what had been left out. Where was the snobbery, the bullying, the homosexuality? 'The programme', wrote the television critic of the *New Statesman*, 'was rather like a documentary about the Western Front which confined itself to telling us what a jolly good spirit there was in the trenches, and how well the officers got on with the men, without mentioning the Germans, trench fever and poison gas.'

Some of the governors who had supported the making of the film, now regretted having done so. David Carey, the legal adviser to the Archbishop of Canterbury, thought the film had done 'a lot of damage' and that those who had questioned the wisdom of allowing the BBC into the school had been proved 'dreadfully right'. More worrying, from my point of view, was an angry letter to the Dean from an influential former pupil urging that I should be dismissed for sanctioning the film's production. Fortunately, the meaningless resolution was in the minutes of the governing body's meeting and its very vagueness made it impossible to pin responsibility for the film on anyone.

The fact that the film made the school so visually attractive despite the over-crowding and played down the problem of drugs must have helped Westminster's competitive position and contributed to the increase in demand for places. Beyond that, it is difficult to say whether the film did much more than make Westminster a topic of dinner-table conversation for a while.

*

I was constantly aware that, although Westminster was well regarded, its limitations made it vulnerable. Eton could shrug off a scandal like a man flicking an insect from his sleeve but, for Westminster, too many drugs cases in the newspapers, combined with high fees and poor facilities, could precipitate a sharp fall in numbers. It was to prevent this happening that I made those changes – good A levels for all instead of Oxford and Cambridge scholarships for a few, the introduction of girls as full members of the school, the rapid increase in numbers – that would help to ensure that Westminster was at least as successful a school as its rivals. Publicity was part of the strategy but to call this a 'notorious PR operation on Westminster' was to credit me with a talent for planning that I did not possess. I just took the opportunities that came along. Publicity did not make Westminster a better school, but it did make it a more sought after one; it did not change Westminster, but it provided covering fire while the changes were being made.

CHAPTER 7

Artful Dodgers and Oliver Twists

Westminster's pupils were the sons and daughters of affluent, professional, middle-class London. Dons from Oxford and Cambridge sent their sons, as did parents from even further afield who wanted their children to have a metropolitan education. But London was the base for the majority, whether they were boys or girls, day pupils or weekly boarders. They were urban children who felt more at home in the King's Road than in the countryside. On one occasion, an exasperated master, whose heart was in the hills, complained to me that a young boy had turned up for an expedition to Snowdonia wearing Gucci shoes and carrying a portable television.

The emphasis on weekly boarding discouraged applications from overseas but London's international community of diplomats and businessmen ensured that Westminster had a cosmopolitan flavour. Not that this would have been apparent to the casual observer. Almost all the boys who entered Westminster at thirteen had been anglicized by a London preparatory school but behind the dark-grey suits and English schoolboy enthusiasms were the grandsons of Prussian junkers and Russian émigrés whose surnames – von Moltke, Kerensky, von Stauffenburg – gave the school list a rich historical resonance. Between 5 per cent and 10 per cent of the pupils were American but, whereas in the eighteenth century the sons of prominent colonists had come by sea from the Carolinas (and returned to fight against their former schoolfellows in the war for Independence), in the late twentieth century, the sons and daughters of American bankers came by underground from Sloane Square.

Whatever the intentions of Henry VIII and of his daughter Elizabeth I, on whose statutes the legal basis of the school rested, the scholars were drawn from the same upper-middle-class families as the town boys. In theory, the scholarships were open to boys from any social background; in practice, they were won by boys from expensive private preparatory schools. If Westminster was not a school for the poor, neither was it patronized by the aristocracy. Though it had once been in favour with the great families, modern Westminster was regarded as unsound by dukes and country squires alike. In Tory eyes, Westminster pupils committed the cardinal sin of appearing to be 'too clever by half'. The 'cocky selfconfidence' that had so irritated some viewers of the Westminster film didn't go down well in Whites or in the shires.

Were Westminster pupils really as arrogant as some of the critics suggested? I suppose they must sometimes have seemed so to strangers. The Dean of Christ Church, to which college many Westminster boys applied, told me that, in Oxford, Westminster's pupils were regarded as 'arrogant and slightly dissipated'. To be educated at the heart of the capital, to worship daily in the Abbey, to be surrounded by affairs of state, to be dissuaded from conforming and told to agree with no one for politeness' sake – these are not the circumstances in which a young boy is likely to develop modesty of demeanour and deference to age and rank. Odd privileges re-enforced the sense of being special; the scholars, for example, were allowed to walk over to the Commons and jump the queue to hear a debate from the Strangers' Gallery.

What was surprising to me was that so many pupils remained unspoilt. Their arrogance was more an intellectual pose than a conviction of superiority. Whereas Etonians, as I discovered on more than one occasion, would ask a question but seldom bother to engage a visiting speaker in argument (any more than their ancestors would have fought a duel with a commoner), Westminster pupils argued for the sake of it, displaying that quality Montaigne condemned in a young man as 'the puerile ambition of trying to appear cleverer because he is different'.

Just how clever Westminster's pupils were I find it difficult to say. They passed exams but that did not prove much. They had above average intelligence but that did not stop them making fools of themselves. They won places at the most selective universities but there was more to it than that. If their cleverness could be distinguished from mere academic success, it was in terms of their ability to make their way in the world, to take their opportunities, to talk themselves into promising situations and out of awkward ones. The nineteenth-century jingle – 'Eton boatmen, Harrow gentlemen, Westminster scoundrels, Winchester scholars' – no doubt did less than justice to many decent and honest pupils, but I had the impression that at Westminster there had always been rather more Artful Dodgers than Oliver Twists.

Youthful idealism was anyway at something of a disadvantage in the 1970s and 1980s. The optimism of the 1960s lingered on into the next decade but it had been discredited. There were still boys and girls who wanted to remove the injustices that disfigured society – that was, I think, how they saw it, as plastic surgery not fundamental change – but they no longer set the tone. Personal ambition reasserted itself; wearing your social conscience on your sleeve went out of fashion. One of the first housemasters I appointed was a keen advocate of community service and could not understand why, as the 1970s wore on, the pupils' enthusiasm for visiting old ladies wore off. He came to see me with furrowed brow; he had been a boy at Westminster and a master for ten years and he had never known selfishness and materialism so rampant.

Worry about pupils' selfishness and materialism frequently surfaced at gatherings of headmasters at this time. But we worried unnecessarily. Human nature had not changed. If the pupils of the 1970s were more inclined to say that they preferred to make money than alleviate poverty in the Third World, at least they meant what they said. What shocked the housemaster was not that the pupils were more selfish and materialistic than their predecessors but that they were less inhibited about showing it.

Those who came to Westminster expecting to find a community of scholars were also in for a shock. Westminster pupils were just as likely to cut corners as their contemporaries in less academic schools.

At 4 p.m. I see a boy who is completing his first year at Westminster. He is seventeen and came into our sixth form from a comprehensive school in Richmond. He is unhappy and disappointed. He came to find a stimulating academic atmosphere but claims to have found only cynicism and opportunism: boys copying one another's work even at this level, and laying hands on advance copies of internal exam papers so that they do not score low marks. He finds the atmosphere far too worldly and too lacking in the intellectual enthusiasm he had anticipated. He says he wishes he had stayed at his former school.

One way in which Westminster pupils did differ from many of their contemporaries in other schools was in their attitude to sport. Those who enjoyed rowing or fencing, football or cricket, took part willingly enough but whether they beat other schools was of no particular interest to the rest of the pupils. There were no heroes at Westminster. No cheering crowds thronged the towpath or the touchline. With the exception of the oarsmen, even those who participated took a relatively detached view of the proceedings, with the result that their opponents regarded Westminster as something of a pushover. I remember seeing a boy in the football XI standing at the side of the pitch talking animatedly with his friends while the match was being fought out in another part of the field. When he saw me, he acknowledged my approach with a wave and trotted off in the direction of the play.

Inevitably, there were, among these metropolitans, some whom the master in charge of games would insist on calling 'physically illiterate'. Natural athletes and games players seldom came to Westminster because preparatory school headmasters preferred to send their stars to schools where games mattered. For some reason, which I was never able to fathom, the more scholarly boys might excel at rowing but almost never at football or cricket. The historian, A. J. P. Taylor, told me that what characterized former Westminster pupils at Oxford was that they could not walk properly. I thought it a curious comment but watching the pupils hurrying to and fro across Little Dean's Yard at the change of lessons, I was struck by the accuracy of his observation. Perhaps there really was a correlation between high intelligence and physical illiteracy.

A headmaster encounters the pupils both as individuals and as a crowd. If he appears to know the crowd better than the individuals it is because he has to. His survival depends on it. He can deal with an individual who defies his authority but if the crowd turns against him, if – as has happened to headmasters – he is booed off stage or shouted down in public, he is a remarkable man if he can recover and continue in office. It was different in the early nineteenth century. Dr John Keate, the headmaster of Eton at the time, was frequently subject to 'a ferment of chatter, laughter, hissing, scraping of feet, booing and yelling' and just as frequently flogged his way out of trouble. It was a time of anarchy and rebellion in public schools and no one expected Keate to resign because he could not make himself heard in Eton Chapel.

A hundred years later, any headmaster who had lost control was finished. In Hilton College, Natal, a school modelled on English public schools, a mutiny in 1953 was only ended when the headmaster made concessions to the senior boys. The trivial nature of the concessions, such as 'the provision of tomato sauce at certain meals', indicated the extent to which the headmaster had been defeated, and why he had to tell the assembled pupils and staff, 'in the circumstances, my duty is clear and I have resigned with effect from the close of the year.'

A silly mistake may also bring a man down. In the 1970s, a new headmaster was asked by the pupils to be an Aunt Sally in the school fête. Thinking it would win him popularity, he agreed to allow himself to be pelted with rotten tomatoes in aid of charity. His authority never recovered and, although he remained for a year or two, his headmastership was effectively ended in one Saturday afternoon.

In his relations with the crowd, the headmaster's goal is not popularity but respect. How he manages to achieve this depends on how he perceives his own strengths and weaknesses. Some headmasters command respect without ever confronting the school as a whole; others, like my mentor, Dr James, command respect despite their dislike of the public occasion. But I needed the public occasions – the weekly Latin Prayers, the morning service in the Abbey – to reassure myself that I was still in control. A demagogue at heart, I exaggerated the importance of being able to sway the crowd and no doubt fooled myself about the extent to which I was successful. My solution to a crisis in my relations with the pupils – it could be caused by an expulsion they thought unjust, or by the introduction of an unpopular policy – was to summon a special assembly and rely on rhetoric to dispel the mood of disaffection. It usually worked, not because Westminster pupils were easily swayed, but because they were too sophisticated and individualistic to coalesce for long around a grievance.

Individualism did not, however, preclude disorder. Westminster pupils were a volatile audience and while they never threatened the hissing, booing and yelling that sometimes greeted Dr Keate, I approached some public occasions with a degree of nervousness. The Pancake Greaze was one. On Shrove Tuesday, selected pupils fought for a piece of pancake in front of the whole school, the Dean and chapter and distinguished guests. It sounds quaint but it was a brutal occasion with no rules, its origins lost in history. Some members of the common room thought it ought to be abolished and refused to attend. I favoured it, despite my anxiety about disorder, on the grounds that – as the Rector of Justin argued – 'you've got to let the boys be animals once in a while.'

From the point of view of crowd control, the Pancake Greaze was a challenge. The pupils understood that this was the one occasion in the year when they could behave like their eighteenth-century forebears – as violent performers and bloodthirsty mob. Those fighting for the pancake became a writhing heap on the floor from which boys emerged with broken wrists and dislocated shoulders. The crowd shouted and pressed forward against the thin line of school monitors. The guests were not certain whether to be amused or horrified.

When the fighting was over, the Dean presented a golden guinea to the boy with the largest piece of pancake. The crowd cheered; the walking wounded were led away. The Dean offered a few thoughts to the assembled company. In Eric Abbott's day, these had been mercifully brief but Edward Carpenter took the opportunity to give the school a lecture in philosophy. 'It was Thomas Hobbes,' he began, on one occasion, as the crowd swayed in front of him like a cobra, 'who characterized man's life as "nasty, brutish and short"'.

It was the presence of outsiders, including parents and governors, that made Shrove Tuesday such a dangerous occasion for the headmaster. If traditional rowdyism became open rebellion and I was unable to bring the mob to heel, my failure would be there for all to see. The secret of survival on all these public occasions, whether rowdy or hilarious, was never to be discountenanced. Whatever tricks the pupils had up their sleeve, the headmaster had to remain in control of himself if he was to remain in control of the situation.

The pupils' ingenuity could introduce an element of hilarity to the most unpromising occasions. Former pupils of Westminster who had achieved some distinction were invited to the school to 'beg a play', that is to ask for a half-holiday. It was a tradition I used sparingly and in doing so offended a number of men who thought that because they had been appointed ambassador or bishop they merited an invitation. One man I did invite was the Nobel Prize-winner for Economics. He was an elderly academic, unaccustomed to addressing school pupils, but it was part of the tradition that, when I had sung his praises, he should reply. As he started speaking, a pigeon appeared. It must have been smuggled in under a boys's jacket. The bird flew up to the roof, then tried the windows and, finding no way out, fluttered down to land on the dais at my side. I assumed an air of unconcern. The speaker droned on, inaudible except to the first few rows, talking about his schooldays at Westminster. With dismay, I realized that he intended taking us through his school career stage by stage. The pigeon took off again and flew over the heads of the school towards the masters. One of the masters must have tried to catch it because there was a crash of chairs and muffled laughter. The speaker continued. The school struggled to keep a straight face. The pigeon settled on the organ at the back of the hall. When, at last, the speaker concluded by asking me to grant a half-holiday, the school exploded with laughter and cheers.

'Was that all right?' He asked as we came out into the sunlight of Little Dean's Yard. 'It went down very well,' I assured him.

Visiting speakers who were regarded as 'pseud', shallow or self-

important got short shrift and there were times when I had to come
to the speaker's rescue. Sincerity and authentic intellectual rigour
commanded respect. Enoch Powell mesmerized the pupils, a
mongoose to their cobra, but the speaker who sticks in my mind is
Isaiah Berlin. He came down from Oxford to speak on 'The Russian
obsession with patterns in history'. The room was crowded and the
day was hot. Berlin spoke fast and made no concession to the age
of his audience. The time for lunch came and went. The pupils
listened attentively to the end. They could distinguish the genuine
article from the superficially attractive and the professionally glib.

My relations with the crowd were not confined to these public
occasions. However remote I may have appeared to some of them,
they could not help seeing me if only because Westminster was
such a small place. I was around the school a lot, dropping in at
breakfast, lunching in College Hall, going into lessons, just wandering around with no particular object in mind. I was no happier
sitting in the headmaster's study than I had been at Taunton. Emo-
tionally, I needed the boys and girls. Just to be near them, to watch
them talking, playing, fooling about, washed away the disillusion-
ment I sometimes felt after a clash with the governing body or the
common room. But I was remote in manner even when I thought
I was being informal. I did my best to put people at their ease but
they seldom were. On some pupils the impression I made was not
an attractive one. 'The head was a ghost-like figure,' wrote one
former pupil in the *Tatler* article I quoted from in chapter 6, 'he
would appear in silence and stand at the back of the classroom,
unnerving the teacher. He was too ominous to be a figure of fun.
One wanted to avoid him.'

My problem was that I wanted to be, if not ominous, then at
least someone with whom it would be unwise to take liberties –
that was the only way the crowd could be controlled – while at the
same time enjoying the pupils' company. I would go out into Little
Dean's Yard on a summer's evening and join in the rough-and-
ready game of cricket they were playing. No doubt the other players
heaved a sigh of relief when I picked up my jacket and strolled away
into the cloisters, but it had not been just a rather selfconscious
attempt to escape the headmaster's role. I had really wanted to play.

On other evenings, I went round the boarding-houses during

prep, calling in at boys' studies, playing the housemaster I had never been. On one visit in the late 1970s, a boy told me in blunt terms that I was out of touch and that I had lost respect because the pupils thought I had little time for them. The criticism struck home not because it was true but because it was the criticism I was most sensitive to. Writing for the newspapers and appearing on television programmes were for me just extra-curricular activities, but I was acutely aware of the danger that the pupils would think the media were my priority.

I redoubled my efforts with them. I held meetings of different age groups where pupils could raise complaints or make suggestions about the running of the school; I took to following a single form for the whole day, sitting at the back during all their lessons, discovering again how exhausting it was to be taught for seven periods on the trot and how slow the moments go when the teacher talks too much.

Most of these attempts to appear less remote were shortlived. I had an idea, tried it for a term or two and then dropped it. Some headmasters would have said that my attempts were ill-conceived, that a headmaster should get on with the job of running the school and not worry about what the pupils think of him. I do not think that I was capable of doing the job that way but I should have remembered from my own schooldays that, however much pupils may complain that they never see the headmaster, they still prefer him to keep his distance. I wanted the best of both worlds: to be aloof and respected but free when I felt like it to play truant from the headmaster's role. As a style of headmastering it could have been disastrous. Fortunately, fear of undermining my authority by being too familiar was usually strong enough to keep the truant in check.

There is a more important question to be asked about the headmaster's relationship with his pupils. Is he merely the custodian of their growing up, responsible for seeing them safely on the road to maturity, or is he trying to influence, change, mould and inspire them so that they will be different men and women than they might otherwise have been? I was ambivalent. I disliked the idea of moulding anyone. 'He moulded their minds after the model of his own,' wrote Samuel Butler of his own headmaster in *The Way of All*

Flesh, 'and stamped an impression upon them which was indelible in after-life'. That was not for me; I wanted no disciples or clones. The Westminster tradition, too, was strongly against anything that might be interpreted as indoctrination. But it would be untrue to claim that I did not try to influence my pupils beyond the routine business of helping them to grow up.

There are few things a headmaster enjoys more than the sound of his own voice. Most of my conscious attempts to influence the pupils were made in the Abbey or Latin Prayers. I took morning abbey twice a week. There was no time for a sermon (the Abbey complained that it lost revenue from tourists if our service went on for longer than fifteen minutes) but it was possible to squeeze in a brief homily between the lesson and the prayer. I was a Christian by upbringing, not by conviction. I was neither an atheist nor an agnostic. I was a deist. I believed that God existed but I had not found him. My homilies tended to dwell, therefore, on how important it was to travel hopefully, to seek God, to face the questions that religion posed. I did not want the pupils to shrug their shoulders and say that religion did not matter, or to be so sure they had found God that there were no more questions to be asked. I preached the virtues of restlessness and insecurity.

Coming out of the Abbey one morning, a senior boy was heard to say, 'I don't mind being compelled to listen to Thomas Cranmer but not to the bees in the headmaster's bonnet.' My theme that morning had not been restlessness but the related one of independence of mind. If there was one theme that I returned to more than any other this was it. One of the penalties of marriage is having to listen to your wife or husband tell the same old story for the umpteenth time. Pupils suffer similarly; masters who stay around for a long time even more so. But I thought this theme so important that it was worth repeating. By independence of mind, I meant the ability to be your own man, to think out your own position and stick to it, to take nothing on trust, to be unpredictable, in the sense that the only thing people can be sure of is that your decision is your own.

Restlessness of spirit and independence of mind were not bad ideals to put before the school but by using the Abbey for this purpose I provoked some of the more pious pupils. They established the Catholic Society to 'counteract the insidious form of "Christianity" which is sweeping the school like one of the nine Egyptian plagues.' The society published a magazine called *Counterblast* whose purpose was 'to encourage to the utmost the maintenance of true religion' in the school. I had no wish to undermine faith or to make it difficult for a pupil to believe, though like Dr Keate, I considered that religious enthusiasm at the age of fifteen was unhealthy. If my religious scepticism influenced the pupils at all, I hope it encouraged them to question their apathy towards religion as well as their easy acceptance of it.

There was no shortage of religious sceptics among the pupils but I never considered allowing them to be excused the morning service. Sceptics, believers, Jews, Muslims, Hindus, even the occasional Zoroastrian, all had to attend morning abbey. Having spent three years studying conscientious objectors, I had no difficulty dealing with boys and girls who said they wished to be excused abbey on the grounds of conscience. If they did not want to take part in the service they could study the memorials. A pupil who is compelled to sit in Poets' Corner for a quarter of an hour has little cause for complaint.

My attempts to influence the pupils were not confined to high-minded matters. There were more down to earth considerations. One was the football team. The boys who played were keen enough but they were too easily intimidated and, with their pink shirts and effete looks, were mocked by the crowded touchline at more hearty schools. I appointed a new master to coach the 1st XI and gave him confidential instructions to encourage the boys to be more aggressive and to make it clear from the start of the match that they were not going to be pushed around.

I was surprised at how quickly the Westminster boys abandoned their languid style of play (I should have remembered that in the eighteenth century, Westminster had been the most violent school of all). Some members of the common room came to see me to lodge a formal complaint. 'Winning at all costs,' their spokesman told me, 'is not the example we want to give the younger boys.' I told them that playing hard and winning at all costs were not the same but they were reluctant to accept that there was a distinction. They thought I was encouraging Westminster boys to be thugs.

Other schools complained too. In October 1983, I made this note in my journal about the Winchester match which had ended in a draw:

As the teams leave the field, the Winchester master approaches me in the grip of an almost uncontrollable rage. I cannot imagine what has got into him. It turns out that he is furious with the hard, abrasive play of our boys. 'I have not seen anything like it since I watched football on Hackney Marshes,' he says. Hackney Marshes? I am at a loss. He accuses our boys of physical intimidation and of 'playing like professionals'. I am delighted because for years I have been trying to persuade Westminster boys to play harder football, as they are so often knocked off the ball by more robust country schools. 'This is not what public school football is about,' the Winchester master tells me as we go into the pavilion for tea. I make soothing noises because he is our guest and is clearly very angry. I can hardly tell him that what he objects to is a direct result of my policy.

My relations with the pupils as individuals began when they took the entrance or scholarship examination. Their parents' initial contact had been with the registrar not with me. At the time of the exam, I interviewed all the candidates: boys and girls, thirteen-year-olds coming from preparatory schools and sixteen-year-olds entering the sixth form. My influence on the selection process was limited to those cases where the candidate was on the borderline between acceptance and rejection. In the other cases, there was no discussion; the examination marks dictated who was admitted and who was not. Every year, there were some boys and girls I would have liked to have admitted and, every year, there were one or two I was sorry to see had done so well. Only once in sixteen years did I refuse to admit a boy who had clearly qualified for entry. At the time of the exam, he alienated every adult he met. He had an older brother in the school. His father was a very rich man. He made no attempt to conceal his impatience at having to submit to a selection process. When I interviewed him, he answered my questions in an offhand manner as though his entry was a foregone conclusion. He

went to a country boarding-school, though what they made of him
I never discovered.

With the borderline cases, I looked for some evidence of originality or strength in one subject even if all the others were weak.
Andrew had excellent marks in Latin and Greek as well as the
lowest Mathematics marks on record; William had high marks in
Mathematics and the sciences but appeared to be incapable of writing a sentence. We took them both. Andrew went to Oxford to
read Classics, William to Cambridge to read Natural Sciences. Both
got first-class degrees. No doubt that is why they stick in the
memory; there must have been other single-subject gambles that
did not come off.

Originality was hard to find. One boy talked his way in with an
extraordinarily detailed account of carnivorous plants, but most
boys on the borderline were punch-drunk from hours of extra
tuition. I was sorry for them. They sat across the table from me,
with dark shadows under their eyes, straining to remember the
answers they had been programmed to give. 'Do you watch any
television?' 'Only news and current affairs, sir.'

The competitive nature of Westminster's entry encouraged this
sort of academic factory-farming. It was impossible to prevent.
Ambitious London parents who had set their hearts on Westminster brushed aside the warning of the preparatory school headmaster and subjected their son to a regime of cramming which,
even if it succeeded in the short run, almost always meant that the
boy was out of his depth when he came to the school.

On the first day of their first term I spoke to all the thirteen-year-
old new boys about the school. I doubt whether much of what I
said sank in. They had too much on their minds, too much information of a more urgent nature to absorb. A few weeks later, I
would take them all into the Abbey at night-time, when we had the
whole building to ourselves, and it was this occasion that I looked
upon as their Westminster baptism, their first immersion in the
mystique of the place. This is where their predecessors had wor-
shipped and where some were buried. We started at the West Door
and walked eastwards, pausing to note curiosities – Ben Jonson
buried standing up because he could not afford the space to lie
down – rather than the memorials of soldiers and statesmen. After

half an hour or so, I let the boys loose to run or roam about the Abbey as they wished. They would never again have such an opportunity. Some, anxious perhaps to establish their scholarly credentials, set themselves to translate the Latin inscriptions; others chased one another among the tombs or climbed up into the pulpit. It was both an introduction to Westminster and a last fling of childhood. 'Sir, sir, is the Abbey haunted?' So, briefly, I became again the schoolmaster I sometimes wished I had remained.

One of the myths that headmasters cultivate about themselves is that they know every pupil by name. There are tricks of the trade that can give this impression but however hard you try, there will always be some pupils in a school of six hundred you know only by sight. You know their names when they arrive and when they are in the sixth form, but in between some will become just faces in the crowd. It is not true that those you know well are the pupils in trouble and the ones who excel. It may also be a matter of chance; there are even pupils you bump into so regularly that you begin to wonder whether it is chance after all, or a deliberate plan to catch the headmaster's eye.

But it was pupils in trouble who occupied my time and filled the pages of my journal. This was not because they were lost sheep and I was their shepherd but because trouble takes much longer to sort out than success. 'Congratulations' is easily said.

Some of them *were* lost, temporarily at least. They took off for a day or a night, as I had done at their age, and were found sleeping on a bench in Sloane Square or on the beach at Brighton. The Brighton police telephoned at two in the morning. 'He tells me he's a pupil at your school,' the duty officer reported, 'will you be coming down to collect him?' When I heard the boy's name, I knew there was no cause for alarm. It would do him good to spend the night in the cells and make his own way back to school in the morning. Pupils who took off in this way – there were perhaps two or three in a school year – were seldom in trouble; they needed a break and slipped back into school life without fuss.

Those who decided to reject Westminster permanently were not in trouble either. They did not like being members of such an élite school. When they said they rejected privilege, I saw no reason to disbelieve them. No argument that parents or teachers put forward could persuade them to stay; on the contrary, the more people insisted on the advantages of a public school education, the more the boys were convinced of the iniquities of the system. They left Westminster and enrolled at the local comprehensive school. Whether their education suffered or benefited is not the point; they had thought out their own line and stuck to it and I, who had so often dwelt on that theme, was in no position to criticize.

The day-trippers and those who rejected Westminster permanently were distinct from those whose disaffection led them into conflict with authority. Headmasters like to identify disruptive pupils as an 'irresponsible minority', just as dictators dismiss their opponents as 'hooligan elements', but troublemakers in a school are not a discrete group operating outside the mainstream of pupil life. The pupils who caused most trouble or who took the greatest risks were friends of those who never put a foot wrong; they had grown up together, they went to the same parties, their parents knew each other well. It suited the school authorities to think of the disruptive pupils as an exception but to their contemporaries they were different in degree not in kind, individuals who had gone too far when anyone could see it was time to draw back.

There were, however, some pupils whose determination to go too far isolated them from their contemporaries. I remember one fourteen-year-old who seemed incapable of keeping out of trouble; his contemporaries did not dislike him but they kept their distance. Nothing he did was serious in itself: he was caught smoking too many times, smuggled bottles of gin and rum into the boarding-house, failed to turn up to lessons or hand work in once too often. Westminster's relaxed attitude to youthful peccadillos worked well for most pupils but not for this one; he went through one warning signal after another like a runaway train, though whether he wanted to crash or just did not register that there was an end to the line, I do not know.

For every pupil we failed, there were many others who found the right person to turn to among the adults in the community. Some members of staff pressed me to set up a tutorial system so that every pupil would have an official 'guide, mentor and friend' in addition to the housemaster, but I refused because I thought that the secret of an effective pastoral network was that it was haphazard. Most boys and girls steered themselves successfully through adolescence and the last thing they wanted was an adult pestering them with offers of help. The great strength of Willie Booth, the school chaplain, was that he was always there when the pupils needed him and not when they wanted to be left alone. Some instinct told him when to be available and when to hold back. It was a rare gift and it enabled him to win the confidence of pupils to a much greater degree than those members of staff who were rather too anxious to be seen to be playing a pastoral role.

On routine matters of discipline, a headmaster's authority is best kept in reserve. I told the staff not to send pupils to me unless the circumstances were exceptional. This did not prevent boys arriving at my door and knocking softly as though they were hoping not to be heard. In most cases, their offence was that they had insulted or defied a junior member of staff. The facts were not in dispute. I felt like the colonial magistrate who greeted the native defendants with the words: 'I find you guilty subject to anything you may have to say in your defence.'

I took the occasion seriously and was suitably stern but it was difficult to be angry. The junior member of staff was learning the trade and needed my support. The boy had gone too far and needed a warning. I told the boy to apologize to the member of staff. He assured me that he would and left the room with the air of a man who was trying to conceal the fact that he had got an unexpected bargain.

Occasionally, the well-tried formula went wrong. Three fourteen-year-olds appeared one winter morning and stood in a row just inside the door. Their History master had sent them. 'Why?' I asked. One of them held out an open exercise book. I took it and read the page. It was a pornographic story, written in three different hands, full of explicit descriptions of male and female genitalia. 'Would you wish me to show this to your parents?' I asked them. They shook their heads. 'Then I shall tear it up and throw it in the wastepaper basket where it belongs.'

I took the exercise book in both hands and tried to tear it in two, but for some reason – my embarrassment, perhaps, or my awareness that the scene was dangerously close to farce – I could not break the cover. The boys stood in silence, struggling to suppress their mirth as they watched their headmaster wrestle with pornography. At last, it came apart and I dropped the pieces into the wastepaper basket. I told the boys to return to class but one of them lingered in the doorway. He wondered whether he could have his exercise book back; it contained all his History notes.

In the room where F. W. Farrar had written *Eric or Little by Little* to inculcate – in his own words – 'inward purity and moral purpose', I did my best not to moralize. A pupil on a disciplinary charge is keen to get out of the headmaster's study as quickly as possible. To keep him waiting to hear his sentence while you pontificate about morality is a waste of breath.

It is also rather cruel. The temptation to be cruel is inseparable from the exercise of power. The tyrannical schoolmaster is a recurring figure in fiction. I do not think I was deliberately cruel or took pleasure in the fear that a headmaster must sometimes strike into the heart of a young pupil. But neither did I sentimentalize the job. If a pupil needed to be expelled, I expelled him. It is impossible to like doing that but there is no point in agonizing over the decision once it has been made. Much better to give what help you can in fixing up another school or a tutorial where the pupil's education can be continued.

Just for the record, those Westminster pupils who were executed for treason, hanged for murder or imprisoned for serious crimes, were not expelled from school, while a number of those who were expelled had successful careers: Robert Southey as Poet Laureate, Francis Burdett as a leading radical parliamentarian, William Markham as a general and ADC to Queen Victoria. Expulsion from school is not the end of a career. Nor should it be. What people get up to in adolescence has very little bearing on how they will behave as adults. Except in the case of illicit drugs. When pupils were expelled for using or providing illicit drugs, the expulsion could accelerate rather than arrest their descent into the drug culture. I expelled one sixteen-year-old who had been selling drugs in the school for a year. When he left my study he said, 'Thanks for everything you have done for me.' I replied that I had not done much. 'No, but thanks all the same.' It was all very polite. Two years later he died of a drug overdose. His mother told me: 'He loved Westminster. It was all we could do to stop him leaving the house at six o'clock in the morning.'

Drug abuse, and the tragedy it might foreshadow, did prey on my mind but it would be naive of me to imagine that the pupils shared my concern. I am opposed to the decriminalization of 'soft drugs' but I am bound to recognize that very few of those who dabbled in such drugs at Westminster came to any harm. It was an incident in their growing up, nothing more. They made the distinction which I did not feel able to make between the occasional, social use of cannabis and active involvement in the drug culture, and they knew from their own experience that one did not necessarily lead to the other. I argued that they were gambling but they did not see it that way; to them, the pupils who became actively involved in the drug culture were stray bullets, not warning shots.

'Congratulations,' I said to the junior boys who were sent by their teacher to show me an outstanding piece of work. Then I spread on the desk top a selection of Maundy money, those small coins the monarch distributes to pensioners on Maundy Thursday. When the Maundy service was held at Westminster, the Royal Mint provided forty sets of coins, one for each Westminster scholar, and these we used to reward outstanding work in the lower forms. If a boy collected all four coins in a set he could sell them at Spink's for a good price. The system favoured those pupils whose teachers believed in it. There was no obligation on a master to send the boy to me and no agreed definition of outstanding work. Some masters complained that the system was unfair, but the advantage of an unfair system was that the prizes went to those who set out to get them, not to those who merely deserved them.

I seldom taught these junior boys because if I was away it would mean asking a colleague to cover for me and I found it much easier to give orders than to ask favours. So I taught European history – French history mostly, from Richelieu to the Revolution – in the upper school where the pupils could in theory be trusted to work on their own. The teaching was the one unforced opportunity to make a partial escape from the headmaster's role, though the subject matter could provide an uncomfortable echo of what had been going on in the school.

Shortly after I had expelled a boy for possessing drugs and reminded the school that this was the automatic punishment, we were discussing Richelieu's attempts to impose his authority on seventeenth-century France. Richelieu had banned duelling on pain of death but a young nobleman had defied him and deliberately fought a duel under Richelieu's window. Richelieu had insisted that he be executed. If he had backed down his authority would have been undermined. 'He had,' I concluded, 'no other choice.'

'Yes, he did. He could have imprisoned him.'

'Not if he had made it clear that duelling was a capital offence.'

'Then he shouldn't have made it clear. It's getting the whole thing totally out of perspective.'

After a few years I started the practice of interviewing members of the upper school at the start of their A-level course and again in their final term. It was a way of identifying the pupils who had become faces in the crowd and of preventing one of them saying in later years when the conversation turned to schooldays, 'The headmaster? We never saw him.' Each interview lasted seven minutes and followed the same formula: how were they getting on in their chosen subjects? What plans did they have for the future? Some pupils, fearing that I did not know them or anxious to ensure that I did not confuse them with the rogue waiting to come in next, introduced themselves. Some had their careers mapped out; others were in no hurry. 'I'm not sure really. Oxford is a possibility. Or I might take a year off.'

The rogues settled themselves in an armchair without being invited to do so. They knew the study well. Their plans for the future reflected their opportunist approach to life – 'I'm keeping my options open' – but I never worried about them. They had learnt how to manipulate the system in their favour; it was one of the benefits of a public school education that did not appear in the prospectus.

The interviews were also my first opportunity to bring into focus the girls and boys who had come into the sixth form from other schools. I seldom got to know them as well as the boys who had come at thirteen. It was not just a question of time; the girls and boys who came at sixteen had left adolescence behind and were unlikely to cross my path on matters of discipline. Those I taught or appointed as school monitors I saw regularly, but the others I saw only occasionally or when they were in the public eye.

Like 'Miss Pretentious 1985'. I never discovered how she managed to alienate so many of her contemporaries. Whatever it was, the lads decided that she should be brought down a peg or two. They chose supper in College Hall, a rowdy occasion from which masters kept their distance. When the hall was full, the lads banged on the heavy oak table to obtain silence. 'We are pleased to announce the award for Miss Pretentious 1985 . . .' The girl was trapped; there was no quick way out of that crowded cauldron. One of the lads climbed over the tables and placed a cardboard crown on her head to the jeers of the mob and the studied indifference of the sophisticates.

The master's common room was outraged (much more so than they would have been if the victim had been a boy). The girl's housemaster insisted that I should send the four lads home but I declined to do so. They were – predictably – extras in a school where most people wanted to be stars. I told them they had behaved like yobs, but I guessed that in thirty years' time they would be among the most loyal attenders at functions for former pupils, seeking, perhaps, the recognition they had been denied at school. The girl took the incident too much to heart. Other girls would have laughed or told the lads to 'fuck off', language that girls used without hesitation when they wanted to throw the more immature boys off balance.

I admired the resilience of many of the girls. They had no intention of being over-awed by the fact that Westminster remained a male society and sometimes, despite its superficial sophistication, a puerile one. But, as with the boys, generalizations are suspect. They were individuals first and girls second. Although headmistresses expressed doubts about whether boys' schools were capable of dealing with 'girls' problems', the problems that arose for sixth formers were mostly academic ones which the boys and girls had in common. If the girls took such problems more seriously, it was because they, rather than their parents, had made the decision to come to Westminster; they regarded the school as a means to an end and were usually less tolerant of bad teaching or the slow returning of work.

I also admired the girls' ambition. One father told me in front of his daughter, 'She needs to meet some boys,' (almost as insensitive as the father who referred to his rather effeminate son as 'my daughter'). But I do not think that meeting boys was the principal motive behind the girls' applications. They were ambitious and Westminster could help them further their ambitions. It was as simple as that.

The sexual lives of the pupils were a closed book. As had been the case with homosexual relationships in the old days, Westminster was too public a stage on which to conduct a heterosexual affair. It is very unlikely that no boys and girls had sexual relations while both were pupils at Westminster but either they were very good at deception or they kept their relationship well away from the school. Though I insisted that, when it came to illegal drugs, the school's jurisdiction knew no bounds, I could not apply that rule to the pupils' private lives. When a father asked me to threaten his son with expulsion if he spent Saturday night with his girlfriend I told him that the matter was his responsibility not mine. The girls appeared to be more sexually aware than the boys and than some of the masters. On one occasion, a bachelor housemaster sent two girls to me because they had been 'disrupting the morning abbey service'. It turned out to be nothing more than laughing together during the hymn, the last line of which was 'O, come quickly'. They had explained this to the housemaster but he had declared their explanation unsatisfactory.

When people ask whether Westminster was a better school for having girls in the sixth form, I reply that I *think* that it was. I am sceptical of those who express dogmatic opinions in favour of mixed or single-sex education. From the pupil's point of view, there are many variables in education and whether the school is mixed or single sex is not one of the more important when compared with the quality of the teaching and the discipline. If Westminster did change for the better, it is not easy to say precisely how. Perhaps Miss Pretentious 1985 provides a clue. She was the exception that proved the rule. Most girls were notably unpretentious and lacking in the intellectual arrogance that characterized some of the clever but immature boys. The rather precious ethos these boys created had never been all-pervading and had probably been losing ground before the girls arrived. But these girls helped it on its way.

The last captain of the school I appointed was a girl, Lynda Stuart. It was not – as some people believed – a parting shot at the traditionalists who argued that only a boy and preferably a scholar could fill that position. I chose the best candidate, who was also the choice of the outgoing captain. But her appointment marked a turning point nevertheless. The girls, though still only 20 per cent of the sixth form, were no longer guests in a boys' school. When one of their number could take the top job it was their school too.

The relationship between the headmaster and the pupil he appoints as head or captain of the school is a close one. In some cases it forms the basis for a lasting friendship but it is usually no more than a temporary alliance of interests. The pupil is glad to have the job. It gives him a pivotal position in the school and there are definite, if intangible, benefits in the contacts he makes and the influence the headmaster is prepared to bring to bear – over entrance to Oxford, for example – on his behalf. I was not close to all the captains of the school I appointed but I believed in paying my debts; if one of them had difficulty getting in to the college of his first choice, I would try to ensure that the difficulty was overcome or that the boy was found a place at another college.

The headmaster is glad to have an ambassador who can interpret his decisions to the other pupils. By the 1970s, the role of captain at Westminster had become largely a diplomatic one; the monitor's tanning pole, cut with notches for each victim, was an exhibit in the school archives. The captains could still exercise power if they chose to do so but it was 'behind-the-scenes' power, the opportunity to influence the headmaster's decision. When I was trying to assess the school's reaction to, say, the decision to expel or not expel a pupil, I listened to the captain rather than the senior masters.

Whether or not the captain followed my agenda or his own depended on his personality and his relationship with me. One who decided to follow his own wrote about it fifteen years later in a Sunday newspaper:

It was really up to myself and the monitors to decide whether people who smoked or drank got disciplined. Our policy was to do nothing about it. At the end of the year, the headmaster said: 'This has been the most trouble-free period.' But the crime level hadn't dropped. It just didn't get reported.

Most captains did not – I think – abandon their responsibilities so wholeheartedly, but even the best captains found that a degree of equivocation was necessary in a role that had something in common with that of a public official in a defeated nation who has to reconcile his loyalty to his countrymen with his need to remain on good terms with the occupying power. Marcus Alexander who held the post for two years (he was only sixteen when he started) became so adept at interpreting my policies to the school and interpreting the school's mood to me that I came to regard him as a colleague. He was a classical scholar who could read people and situations better than most adults. When he left Oxford, he joined a firm of international management consultants and from there, via the Harvard Business School, he set up his own company. Some years later, his Oxford tutor told me that despite his first-class degree Marcus had not been thought clever enough to stay at Oxford and do research. I smiled to myself. How typical of an academic to think that cleverness was synonymous with the ability to do research.

Marcus was the longest-serving captain but not the only one on whose judgement I relied. Sometimes the captain and I would slip away to a pub in Pimlico and sit at a corner table to discuss what should be done about school monitors who were reluctant to enforce school rules (a perennial problem), or how much I should tell the school about the reasons for an expulsion, or whether a rumour that a master allowed boys to smoke in his flat was likely to be true.

The choice of captain was seldom difficult but the disappointment of those who thought they ought to have been chosen could be bitter.

When they left, one third of Westminster's pupils went to the universities of Oxford and Cambridge. Of the remaining two thirds, most went to other universities, to medical schools or to music colleges. But there were two interesting minorities: those who went to tutorials to re-take their A levels (a group Westminster kept quiet about) and those who decided to abandon academic pretentions. Among the latter were some of the more enterprising pupils. Their decision to reject university was probably right. What would have been the point of spending three years studying a subject they were not interested in, alongside people with whom they had little in common, in a university that was bound to seem provincial after life in Little Dean's Yard? Much better to sell their books for a good price to someone in the year below and set off in search of fame and fortune.

I was told that two of these enterprising pupils dined recently at a Paris restaurant. With tears of laughter running down their cheeks, they recalled their Westminster days, how they had spent the small hours carousing while their housemaster was fast asleep and how they had never allowed their academic work to interfere with their social life. The prospect of spending another three years writing History essays was enough to persuade them that university should be avoided at all costs. Now they were in their mid-twenties, one a banker, the other a stockbroker, and both already earning twice as much as the highest paid headmaster. They wore handmade suits and the world was their oyster.

I did nothing to lessen Westminster's traditional emphasis on Oxford and Cambridge. They were good universities and winning a large number of places at them was essential to the school's competitive position. Public school headmasters enjoy dining at the high table in an Oxford or Cambridge college and looking for the faces of their former pupils in the body of the hall. In return, I invited the college admissions tutors to dine in College Hall at Westminster's Election Dinner. It was an agreeable way of doing business. The admissions tutors wanted to attract Westminster's able pupils and we were happy to oblige as long as the college took some of our less able pupils as well. Such academic horse-trading was one of the reasons why Oxford and Cambridge found it so difficult to reduce the number of successful applicants from the leading public schools.

Whether they went to university or not, Westminster's former pupils tended to choose careers that allowed them a degree of independence, the prospect of rapid advancement and a good income. Most of them were not well connected and had to rely on their wits. The Napoleonic concept of a career open to talent was what appealed to them. They did not go into industry because they suspected that most industrial companies prized loyalty above talent. So they became barristers, doctors, merchant bankers, architects, politicians, actors, film and television directors, consultants, journalists and writers. The attraction of the City of London was particularly strong because the rewards and opportunities seemed to go to those who were prepared to gamble on their own talents. Only a handful went into the Church, into schoolteaching, into the civil service or into the armed forces. Fewer than one might expect from a selective academic school chose to spend their adult lives in universities. All these careers had, to a greater or lesser degree, lost public esteem and were poorly paid. They also offered security which was not what most Westminster pupils of the 1970s and 1980s were looking for.

Not long ago, one of the Artful Dodgers hailed me in Regent Street, addressed me by my Christian name and asked me what I was doing now before I had a chance to ask him the same question. He looked as though he was doing very well and I half expected him to offer me a job. Instead, he offered lunch. It was a pleasant hour but towards the end we were running out of conversation. I enjoy meeting the boys and girls who were at Westminster in my time but I do not make the mistake of thinking that we have a lot in common. I want to know what has happened to them, because that is one of the fascinations of being a teacher, and I help them when they ask for help. In my present job in commerce, I come across them more frequently and we exchange business cards, the final step in the normalization of relations. But I am not one of those headmasters who keeps up an extensive correspondence with his former pupils. They are not – thank God – my disciples. They have their own lives to lead.

CHAPTER 8

The Most Demanding Task

A distinctive feature of the headmaster's job is that he has to convince different audiences – the pupils and the teachers (not to mention the parents and the governors) – that he has a magic touch and a special authority. It is not enough for him to be good with the pupils and bad with the staff, or vice versa. Failure to convince one audience undermines his credibility with the other. If the pupils see the headmaster defeated by the staff or the staff see the pupils defy the headmaster with impunity, the circumstances exist in which 'charisma can turn to catastrophe'. Then, like a medicine-man whose bluff has been called, the headmaster must seek another tribe or a different job.

I found the teaching staff more difficult to convince than the pupils. After the first few years, during which I was establishing my authority, I never felt threatened by the pupils. But the reverse was true of the teaching staff; it was in my later years at Westminster that I felt most vulnerable. This was partly because I made mistakes and partly because I stayed too long. Charisma wears off.

I should explain that charisma, as I define it, is not a quality that I possessed. Charisma is in the mind of the beholder. If people believe that an individual possesses exceptional power or qualities they will accept him as a leader; his charisma is real because they think it is. Some charismatic leaders *do* have exceptional qualities; others have charisma thrust upon them by the nature of the role they play. Headmasters do not fit easily into either category. They do not usually have exceptional qualities but neither is their authority based solely on their role. Just to be 'the headmaster' gives you a flying start but, unless you have some of the characteristics of a leader, that initial impetus will soon flag.

Anybody in a position of leadership wishes to convince his followers that he has a magic touch. But, first, he has to convince himself. I found that my confidence ebbed and flowed. There were times when I was supremely selfconfident, almost believing that my hold over the pupils and the staff had a charismatic quality but, at other times, I feared that I was losing my nerve. I was too easily buoyed up by success and too easily depressed by criticism. I did my best to disguise these oscillations, however, because they were inconsistent with my idea of what a headmaster should be.

It was my relations with the teaching staff that made the greatest demands. These were the men and women who looked to me for leadership. When I arrived at Westminster, there were thirty full-time members of staff but, as the school expanded, so did the number of teachers. When I left, there were fifty-one, forty-eight men and three women. Westminster was the sort of school at which people stayed. A few departed to become headmasters but most remained for ten, twenty, even thirty years. That meant that it was an expensive school to run because there were so many men on the top of the salary scale. It was not always the best schoolmasters who became headmasters; fortunately for me, some of the best decided that they preferred to make their career at Westminster. But the combined attractions of Westminster and London meant that some who needed the stimulus of change settled in for the duration of their careers and, in their later years, became more of a liability than an asset.

London also accounted for the unusually high proportion of the staff – about 45 per cent – who were single. Few teachers could afford to live in the city centre and the accommodation the school provided was more suitable for bachelors than married men. There were occasions when I offered a job to a married man but he turned it down and I was forced to appoint a bachelor instead. One view of bachelor masters is that they are often dedicated when they are young but that they develop, in middle age, a certain prickliness and fussiness that makes them difficult to handle. Westminster had one or two who fitted that description but it also had many who did not.

On the question of staff, Dr James gave his protégés this advice: 'Appoint the best and leave them alone.' Every headmaster wants to appoint the best but few are in a position to do so. Westminster paid well compared with St Paul's, badly compared with Eton. The pull of its academic reputation was offset by the problem of finding suitable accommodation. By 1986, the school was accommodating two-thirds of its teaching staff but the demand was always greater than the available supply. The particular difficulties that Westminster faced in attracting staff were exacerbated in the 1980s by the increasing reluctance of graduates to go into teaching. Westminster was nevertheless in a privileged position compared with most schools in the country. If I received only a few applications for a mathematics post, many heads received no applications at all. In those subjects where good teachers were scarce, the leading public schools competed with one another to offer the most attractive remuneration package. The governors gave me a free hand to put a new member of staff where I wished on the salary scale and I was grateful for that. But I had to be careful. If I paid over the odds to obtain a new physics teacher who proved to be interested in nothing but the teaching of his subject, the rest of the staff were angry because they believed, as I did, that there was more to schoolmastering than work in the classroom. They gave willingly of their time out of school, but their goodwill would be eroded if they saw that the men who left promptly at four o'clock were paid more than those who were running out-of-school activities or going over pupils' work well into the evening.

Although the turnover of staff at Westminster was slow, the rapid expansion of the school in the 1970s meant that I had to make a large number of appointments. When I left, only ten of the fifty-one members of staff had not been appointed by me. Although I appreciated the importance of this aspect of headmastering, I did not enjoy it. When I compared notes with other headmasters, I discovered that they shared my lack of enthusiasm. It was just a job that had to be done. Since the choice of sympathetic staff could hold the key to success, it may seem curious that we did not approach it in a more positive frame of mind.

The explanation may be that at this period it was becoming more difficult to make appointments. It was a seller's not a buyer's market, which meant that the headmaster had lost the initiative. Instead of being in a position of power, he was in a position of weakness. However much he might wish to give the impression to the applicants that they would be lucky if he offered them a job, he knew that the boot was on the other foot; it was he who would be lucky if the one good applicant accepted. There were even occasions when the autocrat had to descend to haggling over money with an applicant who realized the strength of his own position. John Carleton interviewed promising applicants over lunch in the Garrick Club. One of his contemporaries, who was headmaster of a school in East Anglia, took over the waiting-room at Liverpool Street station. I preferred to interview on the move, walking through the school buildings or up and down the green in Dean's Yard. If applicants disliked these perambulatory interviews – if they had come with a list of questions in their briefcase and wanted to put them to me in a methodical manner – I was obliged to remain in the study, which seemed more and more like a cage as the afternoon wore on.

Teaching depends so much on personality, I was more interested in how the applicants came across at interview than in their academic qualifications. They would not survive long at Westminster if they did not know their subject, but there was no need for them to be scholars; since many of the pupils would be more intelligent than they were anyway, what mattered was that they possessed a quality of personality that would command the pupils' respect. A colleague of mine at Harrow had arrived from Cambridge with impressive qualifications but, within a few months, the fifteen-year-olds had taken the stuffing out of him. He might have succeeded in any number of other jobs but in the classroom he was a man of straw. The personalities of unsuccessful teachers take many forms but the quality that is missing is always the same – a genuine interest in the pupils. If a man or woman really wants to teach and is genuinely interested in the pupils, he or she will win through in the end. It is the commitment that gives authority not the brilliant mind or the impressive record. That was, I think, what I was trying to assess at interview. The stroll through the school buildings was not just an excuse to be out of the study: it was designed so that we would bump into pupils. I remember one man telling me that he would have preferred to do research but that he was prepared to teach in a school where the pupils were highly intelligent. I suggested a walk. We hit the change-over between periods and for a few moments we were caught in the cross-currents. I could tell he did not like it though he did his best to conceal his distaste. Schoolteaching was not for him.

I advertised vacancies in the newspapers and through the university appointments boards at Oxford and Cambridge. I was as prejudiced as any other public school headmaster in favour of the graduates from these two universities. It was axiomatic that the appointment of too many graduates from other universities was a sign that the headmaster was losing his touch and that the school was going downhill. Such snobbery was not without justification. Prospective parents judged a school's academic and social standing by the strength of its links with the two ancient universities, hence the number of representatives of Oxford and Cambridge on the governing body and the publicity given to the scholarships and places won at the various colleges. The high proportion of staff with Oxford or Cambridge degrees was part of this conscious identification with the two prestigious universities. There was also an implicit assumption that those who had lived and dined in an Oxford or Cambridge college were more likely to 'fit in'.

Laughable or contemptible as these prejudices may seem they did not prevent the leading public schools making good appointments. On the contrary, we took our pick of those undergraduates at Oxford and Cambridge who wanted to teach and had no ideological objection to the independent sector. I do not think these prejudices prevented a headmaster spotting a winner from a different background; everything depended on building the strongest possible team, so that if the right candidate appeared for a particular job, prejudice went out of the window.

As had been the case at Taunton, one of the most important appointments I made at Westminster was to the post of school chaplain. Willie Booth was chaplain at Cranleigh School when I first met him. The headmaster of Cranleigh had invited me to preach in the school chapel one Sunday evening, and Willie Booth joined us for dinner after the service. Westminster needed a chaplain who would be a pastor to the whole school community; after my first meeting with Willie Booth, I was certain he was the man for the job. A few weeks later I offered him the post. The headmaster of Cranleigh was furious; there was a certain etiquette among public school headmasters, he reminded me, that encouraged them to act like gentlemen not football scouts. He was not the first or last of my colleagues in the Headmasters Conference to imply that he regarded me as an outsider.

I had no regrets. Willie Booth joined the Westminster staff in 1974 and stayed for seventeen years. He was our parish priest. He came between us and our sillier selves, he helped the pupils and their families through periods of crisis and sorrow, he christened, confirmed, married and buried us and, by his example, he caused the religious sceptics to think again. He came from a modest background and had been brought up in Belfast. I hate to think what Westminster and I would have missed if I had insisted on appointing a chaplain from Oxford or Cambridge.

Not all my appointments were as successful. In a few cases I made a fundamental misjudgement; I thought the individuals were right for the job but in a short time knew that I had made a mistake. I also made some mistakes when appointing members of staff to positions of responsibility, such as housemaster, from within the school.

Looking back on these decisions, it is tempting to explain the mistakes solely in terms of lack of choice. But that is not the whole story. In one case, for example, I ignored an implicit warning that the man was ambitious to develop his career outside teaching and that he proposed to use Westminster to make the necessary contacts. If I thought the candidate was right, I simply blanked out the doubts expressed by others.

Ignoring other people's advice could, however, have the opposite effect and ensure that I made a good appointment. As at Taunton, my instinct was to go for the youngest candidate, particularly when choosing a new head of department from outside the school. The retiring head of department usually advised me to play safe by appointing one of the more experienced men, no doubt fearing that a young man with energy would demonstrate how much better the department could be run. The more he advised me to play safe, the more certain I was that his department needed shaking up. Westminster acquired some good heads of department this way – and I acquired allies in my attempts to shrug off the influence of the old guard.

In a public school, the leaders of the old guard are usually the senior housemasters. They may be good at their job but a new headmaster is never fully convinced that they are loyal to him. He sees them as the natural opponents of the reforms that he wishes to introduce. The problem is that he cannot change them, at least not quickly. In most public schools, including Westminster, the housemaster's tenure of office was fifteen years. One of my first actions as headmaster was to reduce the fifteen years to ten but, even so, it took a long time to create a team of housemasters who had all been chosen by me. Only when that team was at last assembled did I feel that I was working with colleagues who shared my view of what was required to make Westminster a successful school. Unlike a chief executive in industry, a headmaster cannot put his own men and women into key positions within a few weeks of taking over; he may have to work for years with house-masters and heads of academic departments he would not have chosen.

It would be wrong to give the impression that I had a low opinion of John Carleton's staff; I inherited some outstanding teachers. I did not presume to give these men advice on how to teach but I went into their lessons from time to time to reassure them of my interest and for the pleasure of seeing professionals at work. Their styles differed. Theo Zinn seldom moved from his oak chair which he parked against the door to repel intruders like myself. He sat, wrapped in his gown, his lexicons on the table before him. We could hardly have been more different, he and I. He was the doyen of public school Classics masters and I was the barbarian at the gates. He inspired such loyalty in his pupils that they could properly be called disciples. When he retired, one of them wrote a poem for his farewell dinner which began:

> Olympian Theo! See, the whole school grieves,
> A hundred terms he gave us; now he leaves.

And we must find some form of words to say
How much we feel, how much we mourn today.

Listening to a quiet but incisive exchange between Theo and his
pupils about the merits of this or that translation from the Greek,
as the winter shadows gathered towards the end of afternoon school,
I envied the pupils their encounter with a teacher whose devotion
to his subject transcended all other considerations. Theo taught
well despite me. As a headmaster, I found his defence of Classics's
privileged position exasperating; as a teacher, I found his love of
Classics admirable.

But the pupils I envied most were those who studied English
Literature. Most of Westminster's academic departments had at
least one outstanding teacher; the English department had three.
Jim Cogan, John Field and Rory Stuart were all strong personalities
who challenged their pupils to apply to a poem by Keats or a play
by Shakespeare the same intellectual rigour that was needed to
unlock a complex mathematical problem. They were more
demanding teachers than some of their colleagues and they
attracted more customers. 'The less you demand of pupils,' John
Field told me, 'the more they resent the few demands you do make.'
Pupils flocked to their classes, so much so that the numbers could
not be accommodated. The pupils who found themselves being
taught by other members of the English department protested.

Westminster's reputation for excellence largely depended on the
skills of the outstanding teachers. I had little to do but bask in
reflected glory. But they were in a minority. The test of my leadership was whether I could bring out the best in the remainder of the
staff. How to achieve this, how to help a young teacher believe in
himself, or a tired teacher discover a new lease of life, these were
problems that preoccupied me but which I never fully solved. I
know I brought out the best in some of my colleagues but not in
others.

It is broadly true that public school headmasters rely on the force
of their personalities in their attempts to motivate their staff rather
than taking the more systematic approach favoured by industrial
management. The formal appraisal of teachers' performance is now
taken for granted but in the 1970s it was still regarded as alien to

the traditional way of doing things in public schools. A headmaster *knew* how his staff were performing; the idea that he should set up a system of teacher appraisal to find out would have been greeted with derision, especially by the senior masters. How he knew was part of his charisma. Headmasters, like God, moved in a mysterious way. I do not think Dr James ever went into a classroom at Harrow to see how a master was getting on – but he knew. If young masters had difficulties, he gave them advice. If they continued to have difficulties, they departed for other schools. I never knew whether Dr James sacked them or just made it clear that they had no future at Harrow. I suspect it was the latter.

Dr James was the antithesis of what would now be called a 'hands-on manager'. Despite or, perhaps, because of his reluctance to breathe down our necks, there was nothing we wanted more than to win his praise. He motivated us by giving us the freedom to show what we could do. When I became a headmaster, and particularly when I went to Westminster, I tried to emulate his style. But style is an extension of personality. I found it impossible to resist walking into classes. Some members of staff thought I was checking up on them but my motives were more self-indulgent: it was the familiar urge to get out of the study and to have some contact with the pupils. No doubt I should have been more sensitive to teachers' anxieties. Whereas Dr James gave his staff the feeling that he had confidence in them, my restless prowling must have given some teachers the opposite impression.

I disliked telling people explicitly what their weaknesses were; I preferred to imply disapproval by a coldness in my manner. Jim Cogan once told me that a master felt that I had 'frozen him out'. On the other hand, there were members of staff I stood by when they had difficulties with colleagues or with pupils or hit rough patches in their professional or domestic lives. What motivated me to freeze some out and keep some in was not personal feeling, though there must have been an element of that; it was my conviction that some were good teachers despite their problems and others were not.

A charge commonly laid against the public school headmaster is that he fails to dismiss incompetent members of staff. Even his most loyal supporters among the parents cannot understand why he allows a man or woman who is universally acknowledged to be inadequate to remain on the payroll. From the parents' point of view, no explanation is satisfactory because their children's education is at stake. It does not matter to them that the member of staff is young and will improve or that he is old and has given good service. Nor can they be expected to understand the internal politics that make a headmaster reluctant to act. They suspect that whatever excuses come readily to the headmaster's lips, there is only one reason why he does not sack an incompetent teacher: he does not have the stomach for it.

There were only a few inadequate teachers at Westminster. Some I dismissed. Some went of their own accord. Some of those I dismissed went quietly; others refused to accept that there were grounds for dismissal. Some summoned their union representative; others threatened to take me to an industrial tribunal.

The hardest cases to handle were those of senior men who had lost interest in teaching. Some had been outstanding teachers in their prime – former pupils bore testimony to this – but their powers had vanished and their lessons which once had sparkled were now dull and monotonous. There is nothing a headmaster can do to breathe life into dry bones. I did my best to limit the damage by cutting down the number of pupils affected. It would have been better if I had insisted that these men resigned but it was true, in this case, that I did not have the stomach for it. I never felt sufficiently confident to take the kind of ruthless action that risked turning the common room against me. Instead I tried to ease the dry bones out – 'If you agree to resign, I will ask the governors to boost your pension' – in such a way that the rest of the staff did not feel threatened. It usually worked but it was slow, and meanwhile pupils suffered.

On almost every day my journal records appointments with members of staff. I conducted as much business as possible off-the-cuff during my daily visit to the common room in mid-morning break but a member of staff who wanted privacy and my undivided attention made an appointment. In many cases, he (or she) was seeking reassurance that I appreciated the work he was doing. If he thought I did not, he might start the conversation by saying that he had seen a post advertised in another school and was thinking of applying. It was a recognized opening gambit and it paved the way for a detailed discussion of his teaching, his contribution to out-of-school activities, his satisfaction or frustration with the job and his hopes for the future. These unsystematic meetings were the closest I came to teacher appraisal. Some members of staff kept their distance and instead of asking them to come and see me, I allowed the gap between us to grow.

If a member of staff wanted to pre-empt criticism of his own performance, he might make an appointment, the purpose of which was to direct attention on to some more generalized malaise. One summer holidays, after the A-level results had been published, a head of department telephoned to say that he wished to see me 'on an important matter'. When he came, he first apologized for the fact that he was going to speak frankly and then launched into an attack on the bad discipline and bad manners that – he claimed – had been so prevalent in the school during the previous year. Having set the scene, he mentioned that it was hardly surprising that the A-level results in his department were disappointing. I put it to him tactfully – much too tactfully – that there might be other contributory factors such as poor teaching. He looked surprised at the suggestion and spoke of the difficulty of one department standing out against the prevailing atmosphere of low morale. Bad manners, bad discipline and low morale – where would some members of the common room have been without them?

In some cases I diverted the appointment away from my study to the Athenaeum Club or the Wilton Arms in Belgravia (a pub that was far enough away from the school to keep us from bumping into pupils). Some colleagues, and some topics, did not lend themselves to these more relaxed surroundings, but if a member of staff wanted to get something off his chest it was better that he should do so in circumstances that minimized the employer-employee relationship. It is difficult to stand on ceremony in a crowded public bar. Even so, there were masters who always insisted on formality, like colonial officers who dressed for dinner in the jungle.

I take a senior master for a drink. This morning he said he wanted to see me urgently. 'What about?' I asked. 'Well, basically the common room are very unhappy,' he replied. I drive

him to the Wilton Arms in Belgravia. To my surprise, he
brings an attaché case; it contains two copies of the points he
wishes to discuss, one for him and one for me. I order two
pints and tell him to start. It all boils down to this. At the end
of last term, I told the staff that teaching must continue to the
bitter end; no general knowledge quizzes, no classes let off
early. 'And I supported you one hundred per cent,' he says. 'I
told myself, "He's the boss-man and if that's what he wants,
there's no room for argument."'

I take a swig of my beer. What is he trying to tell me? After
a while it emerges that some masters ignored my instruction
and got away with it. That is what he wanted to get off his
chest: he had done what he was told but the disobedient had
gone unpunished. It has taken almost an hour to reach this
point and all the time he has refused to relax. We might as
well be sitting in my study. He keeps referring to me as 'the
boss-man' in a loud voice as though I was a white hunter and
he was my native servant. The people nearby give us curious
glances.

Some men refused to be diverted. My heart sank when I saw
their names in the diary because I knew that the topic for discussion
would be the same as last time and the time before. What purpose
did these rituals serve in the lives of these men? Typically, they
were former housemasters who had lost an empire and were looking
for a role. They saw themselves and wished to be seen by others as
elders of the tribe and guardians of the shrine. They imagined
people saying, 'If it wasn't for old so-and-so, the school would be
in a bad way.'

Discipline was their topic because it was the issue on which all
headmasters were vulnerable and on which it was easy to imply
with impunity a failure of firm leadership. They enjoyed needling
the headmaster, too; perhaps they resented seeing a younger man
occupying a position to which they had once aspired. One man,
in particular, was a master of the well-placed needle. 'There is
considerable anxiety in the common room,' he told me on one
occasion, 'that the whole system is running down.'

I remember talking to a prison governor about the differences and similarities of our respective jobs. His senior prison officers had much in common with my ex-housemasters; they saw themselves as holding the line against the governor's liberalizing tendency and they enjoyed implying that he was weak on discipline. We chuckled as we compared notes, but the truth was that I took my critics too seriously, worrying that they might represent a wider loss of confidence in my leadership. I felt a sharp anxiety when I heard that one of them wanted to see me, as though he was the headmaster and I was a naughty boy. The irony was that these men were probably more insecure than me; they might even have feared that I was planning to press them into early retirement and have decided that attack was the best form of defence.

To protect myself against the accusation that I had lost control, I was too ready to promise a purge on whatever manifestation of slack discipline had been the subject of the criticism. I was good at launching these campaigns on punctuality, manners and appearance but bad at sustaining them. It was not long before the master of the well-placed needle was back in my study to tell me that my latest attempt to tighten discipline had been 'something of a damp squib'.

The old damp-squib routine was annoying (as it was intended to be) but I asked for it. I should have sent my critics packing but, to the despair of my friends on the staff, I did not do so. Though outwardly calm, I was sometimes nervous within. If stronger head-masters than I could be overthrown by a combination of masters and governors, no one was safe. There was a whiff of paranoia about all this. The thug in me fantasized about dispatching one of the more tedious tribal elders with a combination of punches (I wonder if he guessed what was in my mind as he drew my attention to the sorry state of things) and my bedtime reading was increasingly devoted to the lives of autocratic rulers, such as Peter the Great of Russia, as though I was hoping to pick up a few hints.

In one of our discussions about the nature of leadership, Mike Brearley pointed out that these ritual clashes with the tribal elders had a sexual overtone. The elders wanted to imply that my head-mastership was impotent, hence their talk of damp squibs and systems running down; and my reaction to their criticism was the same as any man's whose virility has been called into question. My relief when one of my critics retired was shortlived; the following term, another senior man stepped into the role. Mike assured me that the same thing happened in all groups, not least in the England cricket team. If an awkward customer was dropped, another member of the team soon took over the part. We decided that in a team or common room there were certain roles to be filled – the awkward customer, the comedian, the prophet of doom – and that some chemistry in the group ensured that no role was left vacant for long.

There are other ways in which the relationship of the headmaster with the staff is characteristic of the relationship between the leader and the group. The individual members of staff are ambivalent towards the headmaster: they want him to be omnipotent and omniscient but they enjoy tripping him up or catching him out; they need him to be approachable but, at the same time, remote; he is both hero and villain and their feelings towards him may be simultaneously friendly and hostile.

I did not analyse the relationship in these terms when I was doing the job but I was aware of ambivalence both in the staff's attitude to me and in my attitude to them. I wanted their loyalty but I often resented the demands they made. I wanted them to believe in my magic touch but I was angry when they passed so many bucks to me. I wanted their friendship but drew back if they tried to come too close.

Whatever ambivalence I felt, I was determined not to show it and having to control my feelings in this way could have disconcerting consequences. Not long before I left Westminster, I attended a management course with other headmasters. In one of the sessions, we were required to role play a scene in which a headmaster was interviewing a young man for a job. Ian Beer, who was then headmaster of Harrow, played the headmaster and I played the young man. But the interview never got far because I had a fit of uncontrollable, almost hysterical laughter, and the session had to be abandoned.

That was one of the rare occasions when the genie got out of the bottle. Most of the time, I had no difficulty being the imperturbable figure headmasters were supposed to be. It was not just an exercise in self-control. Whatever qualities of intellectual and moral excellence I may have lacked, I had stamina. Even though I was too sensitive to criticism and too inclined to oscillate in mood, I absorbed the pressures of the job with comparative ease. Just as my ability to command the public occasion was important in my relations with the pupils, so my ability to absorb pressure was important in my relations with the staff.

Much of my time was spent resolving conflicts, especially those between members of staff or between a member of staff and pupils. 'Conflict resolution' does not appear in the headmaster's job description but, in a society where he is the ultimate arbiter of everyday disputes, it inevitably plays a central role.

A housemaster came to see me because he had received this anonymous letter:

> I hate you and I want you to know that I am not alone in that feeling. Learn how to treat people and maybe there won't be so many people around who hate you. I'd like to cause you as much pain as you cause others, maybe I'll get the chance some day. With all the hatred I possess, from someone who hates you.

The housemaster had his suspicions and wanted me to call in a handwriting expert. I had received hate letters myself and knew how obsessive was the desire to identify the writer; so I contacted a friend at Scotland Yard, who arranged for a handwriting expert to settle the matter. The writer was the boy the housemaster had suspected. He was not a boy who had been in any serious trouble; he was just sixteen and angry. He would forget his hatred soon enough but the housemaster would have allowed speculation to prey upon his mind.

Some members of staff used me to resolve their own conflicts with the pupils. One housemaster created a crisis from the most unpromising ingredients: a broken window pane or a defaced notice was the occasion for a full-scale investigation. He set deadlines for the guilty to come forward and when they failed to do so, told the house in menacing tones, 'This is now a matter for the headmaster.' For some reason his crises always came to a head late in the evening, so that he would appear on my staircase with his tale of woe just as

I was thinking of going to bed. I refused to redeem his empty threats but he never complained. 'Your decision is final, headmaster,' he would say with evident relief and disappear into the night. He had not really wanted me to do anything; he had just wanted an excuse to drop the investigation. In the morning, he would tell his friends in the common room, 'I wanted to take a strong line but the headmaster wouldn't support me.'

Conflicts between two members of staff usually occurred towards the end of a long term when even good men could be intransigent. The master who coaches the 1st VIII has arranged extra outings on the Thames to prepare for Henley Regatta; a housemaster has refused to let his boys take part because they have not finished writing their exams. The two men have exchanged angry letters and each believes he is in the right. They want me to give a ruling. That is the headmaster's job in a nutshell. Whatever the outside world imagines a headmaster does with his time, the reality is that he spends much of it giving rulings, often on matters of a trivial nature. I was impatient that grown men needed me to sort out their quarrels, but I would never have delegated to anyone else the authority to do so.

A letter which began 'The chicken at today's lunch as well as looking revolting was cold and uncooked,' heralded a different kind of conflict that, however trivial, was potentially dangerous. When a member of the staff was at loggerheads with the school bursar, both parties believed that they were entitled to the headmaster's support. An attack on the bursar might be an oblique attack on the headmaster; if the headmaster did not overrule the bursar, the member of staff would return to the common room and ask, 'Who is running this school?'

At Westminster, the headmaster was the chief executive and the bursar was the finance director, with responsibility for financial management and for the non-academic functions such as catering and building maintenance. It looked like a clear division of responsibility but, in practice, it was nothing of the sort. The bursar reported to the governing body; how far he came under the headmaster's authority was never made clear. I could complain to the bursar about the revolting chicken but I could not insist that he sacked the chef or spent more money on school food.

The bursar was also clerk to the governors. Close contact with the most influential members of the governing body encouraged him to adopt, like Malvolio, a more distant attitude to members of the teaching staff. Since bursars tended to be former officers of the armed services who were used to working in a clearly defined hierarchy and teachers were often sensitive to any suggestion that their status was inferior, the potential for conflict was considerable.

The bursar when I arrived at Westminster was a former Group Captain in the Royal Air Force, William 'Simba' Lyons. A large man with a flushed complexion and military moustache, he had summoned me to the Jerusalem Chamber for my final interview with the governing body and it was he, not the chairman of the governors, who had written to tell me I had the job.

In my early years at Westminster my relations with Simba were strained. He never presumed to comment on educational matters but we had our bitter disagreements nevertheless. He fought tooth and nail against my proposal to set up a joint advisory body of governors and teaching staff to review salaries and conditions of service. I wanted to bring governors and members of staff together; he wanted to keep them apart so that his own position of influence would not be undermined. When he retired in 1978 (he was over seventy but had managed to keep his age a secret and no governor had had the courage to ask), he was given a farewell dinner in the Jerusalem Chamber at which I seconded the proposal of his health. I was so pleased that he was leaving, I had no difficulty being generous.

Then, three years later, Simba's successor died in office and the governing body asked Simba to return until a new bursar was appointed. My initial dismay at the return of my old adversary soon gave way to gratitude as, this time round, something approaching friendship developed between us. We had never talked much except on official business; now we found time to discuss our respective roles. To my surprise, he had a shrewd eye for the absurdities of school politics and was cheerfully indiscreet about governors and members of staff. When he described one particularly self-important senior master as 'a silly old bugger', I was taken aback. If only I had known that he found such men as infuriating as I did, what allies we might have been.

A new bursar was appointed. Some months later, the governors gave a second dinner in Simba's honour, this time at the Carlton Club. When I arrived, I found an ambulance parked outside. Simba had had a heart attack in the taxi and died shortly after in Westminster Hospital.

I went into the club and found the governors gathered in a private room, unsure whether to disperse or go ahead with the dinner that had been prepared. The bishop expressed the view that we should disperse immediately but this was greeted with little enthusiasm. Some of the governors had come a long way and the prospect of a good dinner was not that easily dismissed from the imagination. So we sat down and enjoyed the meal. When the last course had been cleared and the port had been circulated, the bishop invited us to stand in silence. How Simba would have laughed. We stood with heads bowed, our port half-drunk, our cigars smoking in the ashtrays, while the bishop prayed for Simba's immortal soul. When he led us in the Lord's Prayer, one or two governors stumbled over the half-forgotten phrases but we arrived at the 'Amen' more or less in unison. Then we sat down and resumed our conversation.

My relations with the staff were also conducted in the formal setting of meetings: common room meetings at the beginning and end of term, heads-of-department meetings once a month, housemasters meetings every Thursday evening between six and seven, and meetings of the numerous *ad hoc* groups, committees and working parties that I set up to wrestle with specific issues.

The meetings served a number of different purposes: to exchange information; to give members of staff a chance to put forward their ideas; to debate the advantages and disadvantages of a particular policy; to allow frustration and aggression to be released in a controlled environment; and to demonstrate to those who doubted it that some problems remained as difficult to solve, however often they appeared on the agenda. The one purpose the meetings did not serve was to make decisions. I made the decisions, sometimes at the meeting, more often when the meeting had dispersed. My policy was, 'Thank you for your advice, I will let you know my decision', though I do not think I ever put it in those words. I never took a vote because I did not wish to be bound by the result.

In sixteen years, no one questioned or challenged this method of government. That was not because the members of staff were docile – they were exceptionally lively and independent-minded – but because they had been brought up in the public school world and accepted that this was the way such schools were run. The head-master was treated as 'the boss-man' because like a general or a football manager or a film director, it was his plan they were all working to and it was his head on the block if things went wrong. The fact that the bursar held the purse strings, and the governing body had to approve major expenditure and changes in policy, in no way modified the expectation of the staff that I would make the decisions both about the day-to-day running of the school and about its future development.

Just as I was anxious not to be thought weak on matters of discipline, so I was determined not to be thought indecisive on matters of policy. What more damning criticism of a headmaster could there be than that he was unable to make up his mind? My methods of reaching decisions varied. If it was an issue that I did not think important, I allowed myself to be swayed by public opinion. If I knew what I wanted and I thought I could get away with it I presented the decision as a *fait accompli*. If a minority in the common room pressed me to make a decision that I knew would not have general support (even though the minority claimed to speak for the common room as a whole), I declined to do so unless they were prepared to put the matter on the agenda for a full common-room meeting. Outmanoeuvring unrepresentative minorities was an important part of the job.

So was obtaining a degree of uniformity among housemasters. I tried to centralize power in my own hands to avoid the friction that so often occurred when housemasters interpreted the rules in their own way. At other schools, notably Eton, the housemasters had continued to act as autonomous barons who were able to resist the centralizing tendency of headmasters, but at Westminster the housemasters were idiosyncratic rather than baronial. I was in favour of housemasters having a distinctive style and setting their own priorities. If one housemaster was an enthusiast for music and drama, while his neighbour exhorted the boys and girls in his house to spend their free time working with disadvantaged children in the

East End, no harm was done. But if one housemaster punished a boy for not going to bed on time, while his neighbour turned a blind eye to boys of the same seniority staying up until the small hours, the pupils and their parents might reasonably ask what the school's policy was. My response was to make more of the housemasters' decisions for them. I whittled away their discretionary powers because I was impatient with disputes caused by different interpretations of the school rules.

The weekly housemasters meeting was my opportunity to see that local idiosyncracies did not get out of hand. It was also a safety-valve:

The housemasters meeting follows a pattern that is familiar at this time of term. We are due to discuss the changes in Oxford and Cambridge entry but as we are settling down someone comments that one of his new boys finished games so early this afternoon that he had time to go home for tea even though he is a boarder. Why are games allowed to finish so early? Why are some members of the staff allowed to opt out of supervising games? Is our credibility as a boarding school likely to survive if parents find their boarding son arriving home for tea in Kensington on a games afternoon? We are soon off on a wild goose chase through the complex maze of problems that face a school that tries to be a country boarding-school in the middle of London. I let it run because there is clearly a lot of energy and feeling to be released. Changes in Oxbridge entry can wait till next week.

On most academic decisions, I took the advice of the director of studies. I inherited as director of studies a very clever man whose explanation of how the timetable worked I could not understand. When he departed, taking the secret of his timetable with him, I found successive directors on whose clear minds and good sense I could rely to help me reform the Westminster curriculum. There were some changes which they initiated and I endorsed and others where I dictated the end and they recommended the means. This kind of collaboration with key individuals was my favourite way of reaching a decision; larger gatherings never seemed to get anywhere, though they did provide an opportunity for those not directly involved in decision-making to cross-question those who were.

My decisions to change Westminster were not part of a grand design. I had no vision of how things ought to be, just a sense of what was needed if Westminster was to be competitive. I admired individuals who could relate all their decisions to a master plan. When I had a sabbatical in 1983, I spent part of it in Thailand at the invitation of the film producer, David Puttnam. He was setting up his film, *The Killing Fields*, and, knowing my enthusiasm for the cinema, he suggested that I should join him. I attached myself to the director of the film, Roland Joffé. He was also a man who spent the day making decisions, but his decisions were all related to his vision of what he wanted the film to be. He had worked out in detail how each scene was to be shot and had made sketches in his notebook of the camera angles, so that when he consulted his professional colleagues – the cinematographer, the art director – he could measure their ideas against his own. I envied him his ability to know exactly what he wanted.

A headmaster cannot plan every scene; most of his bad decisions are in response to problems that catch him unawares. Westminster, with its crowded site and expensive location, did not lend itself to the sort of five-year building plan that allowed some public school headmasters to indulge their delusions of grandeur. Even so, I should probably have had a clearer idea of what sort of school I wanted Westminster to be. Making it more successful than its rivals was a strategy for survival, both for the school and for myself, but it was hardly an ideal.

After the first flurry of changes, I made the mistake of setting up a committee meeting under someone else's chairmanship. It produced a report which began:

From discussion with a number of members of the common room it is evident that there is a lack of confidence about the general control of the school. Our priorities are not clear because they have been blurred by too many changes and experiments in the timetable which has caused frustration and a lack of conviction and professionalism.

After that I chaired all the committees myself. It was not an aspect of the job I particularly enjoyed but the desire to be in control was stronger than my weariness with the kind of repetitive discussions that committee meetings so often produced. By far the best discussions I had with members of my staff were the informal ones, over dinner, in the pub and on the last night of term when, under the guise of policing the pupils' escapades, we gathered in the common room and talked into the early hours of the morning. I loved those end-of-term occasions when we were relaxed with wine and the prospect of holidays, and men whose relations with me were distant sank into armchairs at my side and joined in the discussion. How courteously we listened to one another's arguments. How readily the pieces of Westminster's complicated jigsaw fell into place. Meanwhile, the pupils crept out of their boarding-houses to paint the railings pink and tie pyjamas to the Abbey roof.

It was because I disliked one-to-one meetings in my study that I spent more time in the common room than most headmasters. Too much time some masters would have said. How could they bellyache about the headmaster if he might walk in at any moment? Every Monday morning during break I made announcements in the common room. It was also an opportunity to give members of staff the sort of reminders – about being punctual for their classes, for example – that would have sounded smallminded on paper. It was not an opportunity for debate or for raising controversial issues, though there were members of staff who tried to use the occasion for this purpose.

I sometimes dreamed of having a perfect team, with no weak members, but I knew that this was no more likely than that the staff would have a perfect headmaster. A headmaster is in the same position as a football manager: no sooner has he found a first-class striker than his goalkeeper is offered more money to move to another school. The football manager is expected to make the best use of the talents at his disposal and so is the headmaster. Despite the fact that my policies and personality alienated some members of staff, I tried to bring out the best in this common room of diverse talents. What sticks in the memory, however, is not their talent but their willingness to undertake roles for which they had little or no aptitude. Physically illiterate members of staff were to be found refereeing, umpiring and coaching. Men and women who had never seen a fell, let alone walked on one, happily went on expeditions as supporting cast to the men whose hearts were in the hills. There were very few who did not regard it as normal to work long hours without complaint, to cover for absent colleagues without hesitation and, in term time, to put the school before their family and home. Teaching was not a job they went to in the morning and left behind them at the end of the working day. It was their life. Though it may sound trite or even hypocritical in view of the battles I fought with some of them, I think of myself as fortunate to have worked with men and women for whom teaching was a true vocation.

CHAPTER 9

Parents and Governors

An analysis of the occupations of some Westminster parents in the 1970s shows the predominance of successful businessmen, doctors, lawyers, engineers and academics, with a seasoning of diplomats, journalists, architects and actors. Since the 1870s, the most striking change had been the rise of the company directors and the virtual disappearance of the clergy and the armed forces.

Company director/executive	19	Architect	4
Medical/dental	16	Banking	4
Law	11	Theatre/cinema	4
Engineer	10	Chartered accountant	3
Academic	10	Politician	2
Journalist/writer	7	Public relations	1
Civil servant	6	Clergy	1
Diplomat	4	Armed forces	1

———

103

The above occupations are taken from the registration forms completed by the parents; in most cases, it is the father's occupation that appears, even though a significant number of mothers had careers of their own. Despite this limitation, the analysis gives a reasonably accurate picture. It does not reveal much about their personalities, but the way parents reacted to the school and to the headmaster could be an extension of their professional lives as well as a reflection of their characters. Barristers whose boys were in trouble sat on my sofa with a sheaf of papers on their knees and addressed me as if I were a jury. A Shakespearian actor whose son I proposed to send home for a few days quoted *Coriolanus*. It would not be a question of the school rejecting his son, he told me, but of his son rejecting the school. Like Coriolanus addressing the people of Athens, his son would say, 'I banish you.' The actor had a fine, resonant voice so that the words 'I banish you' seemed to remain audible as we sat in silence looking at one another.

Only 4 per cent of Westminster parents were former pupils of the school, compared with 40 per cent at schools such as Eton and Ampleforth. Westminster's alumni were not noted for their sentimental attachment to the school. On the other hand, Westminster benefited from the large number of foreign mothers who would have nothing to do with the country boarding-schools at which their husbands had been educated. About a quarter of the pupils had parents who were divorced or separated. There were many variations on this theme. One boy was told by his mother when he was fifteen that the man he had always believed to be his father was not his father after all. Some parents were effectively separated because careers (or, in a few cases, prison sentences) kept them apart. When a film director's son was in trouble, his father flew in from Hollywood, gave instructions for his son to follow a regime of all work and no play, and flew out again, leaving his wife, who was based in London, to see that his instructions were obeyed. Even when parents were together, it was not unusual for one of them to take all responsibility for contact with the school, with the other parent seldom, if ever, appearing.

Relations between parents and schools had changed profoundly since I was a child. When my brother, Angus, and I went to boarding-school, we did not expect to see our parents again until the end of term unless we developed acute appendicitis. As far as I can tell, our parents' only information about how we were getting on came from the brief, almost monosyllabic comments on the end-of-term reports, and from what little they could glean from our carefully edited answers to their questions during the holidays. They loved their children but they belonged to a generation which regarded education as a matter for schools not parents.

Sending children away to boarding-school remains fashionable among the English middle classes but keeping parents at arm's length from education died what seems to have been a natural death in the 1960s. By the time I went to Westminster, it was accepted wisdom at all but a very few public schools that parents should be consulted, informed, invited to discuss their children's progress with teachers, welcomed at school functions and generally treated as though they had something to contribute especially, it has to be said, when the school was launching an appeal for funds. Education, we discovered, was a partnership between home and school.

If I sound sceptical, it is only because I was aware of the exceptions to the general rule. Westminster had a number of over-ambitious parents whose sons and daughters would have benefited from a little more parental neglect. I was also sceptical about the concept of parents as customers or – in the jargon of the 1980s – consumers. Parental complaints could be useful ammunition for keeping lackadaisical members of staff up to the mark or for re-enforcing the case for changes of policy that I was proposing to introduce. But I was not a shopkeeper and I did not believe that the customer was always right.

Nor was I a lobbyist available for hire. Parents who tried to pressurize me into pulling strings at Oxford and Cambridge got short shrift and did not like it. One grandfather whose repeated attempts to persuade me to open Oxford's doors for his grandson were unsuccessful, wrote, 'Headmaster, for years you have treated my daughter and myself with nonchalance and contempt,' but his anger was misdirected. If he wanted strings pulled at Oxford, he would have to do it himself. Other parents did and were adept at using the establishment networks.

I lunch at Brooks with the father of a sixth former. He met the senior tutor of his old Oxford college at Newmarket, when both were enjoying the corporate hospitality of a merchant bank. Between races he arranged for his son to visit the college and meet the Master, and now he wants me to follow this up with a letter of recommendation.

Oxford colleges, though not Cambridge ones in my experience, were prepared to accept financial sweeteners but, in general, most colleges at both Oxford and Cambridge were impervious to appeals based on family connections and the old-boy network. If you must give places for reasons other than merit, it is better to exchange them for cash in hand than for the uncertain benefits of influential friends.

I would have sold a place at Westminster if the price had been high enough, but it never was. 'Would a gift help?' a rich Texas oil man asked when he came to see me about his son's entry to Westminster. At least it made a change from the English approach of pulling rank. Three prime ministers tried their hand at assisting a candidate for entry. Alec Douglas-Home recommended a boy from Bangladesh to whom I gave a place. Edward Heath appealed unsuccessfully against the rejection of a boy who had failed our entrance exam. Harold Wilson invited me to 10 Downing Street. Marcia Falkender, who ran his private office, had sought entry for her two sons to our preparatory department. Since they were bright and likeable boys that presented no problem. I was summoned to Downing Street, nevertheless. Wilson greeted me warmly and we talked for an hour about history and politics, about his own schooldays and about his belief that King Arthur was buried on the Scilly Isles. Then he stood up and said goodbye. That was all. The boys' entry to Westminster was never mentioned.

I tried to avoid seeing prospective parents – that was the registrar's job – but those who slipped through the net provided a pleasant diversion from the daily round:

A Nigerian chief appears, blacker than a moonless night and so garrulous I can hardly get a word in. He has two wives and eighteen children. He wants us to take one of the boys, who is thirteen. The boy is called Gowon, for which the chief apologizes profusely, the name having been chosen when General Gowon was head of state. I mention that I met Gowon in Lagos and that since his fall from power we have remained good friends. 'Oh, a first-rate man,' says the chief without batting an eyelid, 'a really first-rate man.'

Once a boy or girl was in the school, I made no systematic attempt to get to know their parents. I met most of them at the parents 'parties' when they came to consult teachers, or at the meetings I arranged to discuss specific topics such as careers and university entrance. Some parents went out of their way to build a relationship, inviting us to the theatre or to dinner; I enjoyed their hospitality but gave their children no favours. Others clearly regarded the headmaster as someone to be avoided at all costs. Some parents were too in awe of the headmaster to come to the functions, others reckoned it would be a waste of time because they thought I was too remote to know their child. Some came to complain, others because I had summoned them to discuss their son's work or behaviour. The parents I got to know well, therefore, were those who took the initiative in the relationship, and those whose wayward offspring brought us together.

A mother comes to see me. She allowed her sixteen-year-old son to give a party on Saturday night at their home in Chelsea. He invited far too many people and as many again appeared uninvited. She called the police who cleared the crowd outside the building but those inside were not so easy to dislodge. She was shocked by the behaviour of the boys and girls from Westminster and elsewhere: swearing, drinking too much, stubbing their cigarettes out on the carpet, abusive when told to go. I am angry with her for allowing the party in the first place, particularly when I hear that her husband was away on business.

The teenage party out of control was a parental nightmare but still some parents allowed too many people in, provided too much alcohol and then went out for the evening leaving an au pair or an older sibling in charge. Having teenage children of our own helped to keep my criticism of such parents within reasonable bounds. It also raised the tricky question of which role I was playing. When I collected Siobhan or Penelope at a late hour, there was tacit understanding that I was a father not a headmaster. As I picked my way through the debris and the recumbent shapes, an invisible figure went before me carrying a white flag of truce. The parents were usually sitting in the kitchen trying not to look as though they had been taken hostage. 'Ah, Dr Rae.' There was a note of ambivalence in their greeting, as well there might be.

When a pupil had to be expelled, I saw the parents to give them the news. Because it was potentially such a difficult occasion, I tried to keep it low key and brief.

After Latin Prayers, I see the parents of the two boys who are to be expelled. The first father tells me that when he heard what his son had done, he thought about it calmly in the office; then he went home, summoned his son into the study and hit him hard in the face. 'I have not done that for many years,' he adds. The boy is sixteen. The next parents are sadder. They are separated and the mother is desperately tearful. She had to bring up the boy on her own. Father talks in a detached way about finding another school but mother cannot accept that it is fair for her boy to be expelled. The separation hit him hard. 'He has never had a chance,' she says.

It was easy to feel sympathy for this mother but hard to find the words in which to express it. When I said I was sorry things had turned out this way I meant it, but even as I spoke the words I was thinking that they were a convenient formula for bringing the interview to an end.

Headmastering re-enforced my inclination to keep my emotions to myself. As with the pupils and the staff, so with the parents: I did not want to give too much away. The danger of giving way to unguarded emotion was one of the hazards of a headmaster's life, though not always a disagreeable one.

A mother comes to see me about her daughter's university entrance; mother is disconcertingly attractive and I have difficulty concentrating on the matter in hand.

I found it hardest to control the temptation to hit back at what I thought was unfair criticism. In a competitive market, the parents knew exactly how to make their dissatisfaction felt. They played upon the rivalry between headmasters. All that was required was some taunt along the lines of 'They do these things so much better in other schools.'

An awkward interview this morning with the parents of a sixteen-year-old boarder who is at odds with the school over a hundred and one breaches of the rules and is now refusing to turn up to all lessons. I have had enough, particularly as the boy is leading others into his alienated world and frightening younger boys with his aggressive punk passage through the school. But his parents don't see it that way: to them he is a fundamentally good boy who has been turned sour by our petty regulations and unsympathetic handling. I say that one more incident will be the last straw; they say they will withdraw him anyway and send him to a crammer. 'He had a place at St Paul's,' his father tells me on the way out. 'I wish now we had taken it. Everybody says the new man there is doing a wonderful job.'

It is a part of every school's job to help the parents take the strain of the pupils's growing up and at Westminster the partnership usually worked well. School and parents did not always agree or feel the need to tell each other everything. On the contrary, one of the secrets of a successful partnership between home and school is that they do *not* tell each other everything. Growing up is a private business. An adolescent needs his secrets and needs to be able to do things at school that parents know nothing about and vice versa. It would never have occurred to me to tell the parents about their sons' peccadillos, any more more than it would have occurred to parents that they should tell me what their sons or daughters got up to at the weekends and in the holidays.

Some parents knew, or thought they knew, more about the secret lives of Westminster pupils than I did and had an annoying habit of dropping hints at dinner parties. 'I could tell you a thing or two, Dr Rae,' one mother assured me. The other guests fell silent hoping to hear some scandal. But the details were seldom forthcoming. I did not blame the parents for their reticence. I felt under no obligation to tell our childrens' schools more than it was necessary for them to know. When our daughters were at Westminster, what I knew as a father was kept separate from what I knew as a head-master.

When the partnership between parents and school proved inef-fective it was not because of a failure of communications (that favourite scapegoat of the period) but because the school or the parents had made an error of judgement.

X's father comes to see me. The boy, who is sixteen, has run away from school and home. I gather he is sleeping on the floor of friends' houses and moving on again in the morning like an agent on the run in enemy territory. Father and I stare into the flames of the gas fire, brooding on the problem of children. We have known each other for twenty years and have large families of much the same age. 'The school has made a balls-up of X's education,' he says at last. That is one way of putting it. Father is a bibliophile; son does not give a fig for books. Father insisted that boy should go on the fast stream to O level; I made the mistake of giving in to his pressure. The boy switched off altogether. He has friends outside the school who wear leather gear and ride motorcycles.

Although we made some lasting friendships with the parents of Westminster pupils, the alliance between school and parents is a temporary one. On the whole parents do not like headmasters and are not sorry when the partnership is dissolved. Just as it is a plea-sure to meet some former pupils, so it is to meet some former parents. But I suspect that most parents would prefer not to renew the relationship. Shortly after leaving Westminster, I saw a parent I had known well walking on the pavement towards me. When he realized who I was, he turned abruptly into a shop entrance. What he had not noticed in his haste was that the shop was shut, so that as I walked past I saw him standing with his face to the closed door like a small boy who had been told to stand in the corner.

There was no formal contact between parents and governors. From time to time, parents were elected to the governing body but in their own right, not as parents' representatives. When I left West-minster in 1986, five of the eighteen governors were current or former parents, including Edward Carpenter, the Dean and chairman, whose two sons had been in the school. There was, at Westminster, a higher proportion of governors who saw the school from the parents' point of view than in many other public schools or, for that matter, in many state schools, but it was by chance not by design.

The school had little or no say in the appointment of half its governors. Not only was the Dean automatically chairman, but the Dean and chapter elected two other governors who were invariably canons of the Abbey. The Dean of Christ Church, Oxford and the Master of Trinity College, Cambridge were *ex officio* governors. The senior members of these two colleges also had the right to elect one of their number to sit on Westminster's governing body, as did the Royal Society. And one governor was nominated by the Lord Chief Justice.

These nine governors elected nine others. Members of the teaching staff could choose any one of the governors to represent their interests and in practice that governor represented my interests too. Throughout my time at Westminster, that role was filled by Burke Trend. The flavour of the governing body was masculine (the first woman governor was elected in 1983), elderly (the average age was over sixty), and despite the presence of four clerics, secular. About half the governors were former pupils of the school; most of them had been elected on merit and did not engage in the sort of intrigues against the headmaster that characterized the old-boy cliques on some other governing bodies. Former cabinet ministers and Nobel prize winners had better things to do. There were, however, one or two governors I did not trust because I knew they would not hesitate to join any move for my dismissal.

My relations with the governors were friendly but, with the exception of Edward Carpenter and Burke Trend, I would not have counted them as close friends. In contrast to the governors of Taunton, they were men of the world who had seen too much in public life to panic at the first unfavourable reference to the school in the newspapers. Their worldliness made my life easier. But it was also a weathervane of their attitude to me; when wordly men started to worry about boys' shirt-tails not being tucked in, I knew it was time to look for another job.

Public school headmasters enjoy an independence that most heads of state schools are denied. The latter have to accept that governors have the right to be involved in the appointments of members of staff, a degree of interference that would have been totally alien to most of Westminster's governors. The traditional independence of public school headmasters owed much to Dr Arnold, who had refused to take over the headmastership of Rugby in 1828 unless the governors gave him an assurance that they would not interfere in the administration of the school. The independence I enjoyed also owed something to Westminster's long-established reputation. The governors may not have liked everything I did, still less everything I wrote, but they were confident that the school's reputation was robust enough to withstand the rough handling some people thought I gave it. It would have been a different story if numbers had been falling but even those governors who disapproved of my style were forced to admit that it did not frighten the customers away. The critics bided their time.

The governors met four times a year in the Jerusalem Chamber, once part of the Abbott's lodgings and the scene of various historical events from the death of Henry IV in 1413 to the writing of the Authorised Version of the Bible in 1611. Overburdened by history and by the heavy lunch that Simba provided, the meetings of the Westminster governing body seldom took flight. Much of the time was taken up with the report of the executive committee which its chairman went through at a snail's pace. The combined effect of Sir Henry Chisholm's monotonous, almost inaudible voice and the fumes of the claret was too much for some of the governors. All round the table, men struggled to look as though they were still awake. I was reminded of that scene in *Beau Geste*, where the hero props up the dead men in the embrasures to give the impression that the fort is still being defended. Rab Butler would close his eyes and bow his head soon after the meeting started but he was not asleep, just dozing. When Edward Carpenter asked, 'What does the Master of Trinity think?' Butler would open his eyes, contribute a penetrating comment and then close his eyes again.

From time to time, an issue such as the Pope's helicopter or the boys' shirt-tails provoked a lively debate but, for the most part, it was routine stuff about the finances and the statutes. When Sir

Henry retired, the report of the executive committee took on a new lease of life but discussions on the statutes remained as dull as ever. Most of these discussions were unnecessary and only took place because one of the governors cast himself in the role of keeper of the statutes. Sir Reginald Sharpe was a former colonial judge who had opposed my appointment and took every opportunity to imply that I was exceeding my powers. He was the one governor I felt to be consistently hostile. The other governors humoured him. It was all very English – Sir Henry droning on inaudibly, Sir Reginald wasting time with his legal nit-picking and no one wishing to give offence by suggesting that Sir Henry should speak up and Sir Reginald shut up. Edward Carpenter had sufficient skills as chairman to ensure that the business was completed before the arrival of tea, but I was amazed that busy men put up with Sir Henry and Sir Reginald for so long.

The executive committee met eight times a year. When Sir Henry retired, I persuaded the new chairman to allow two members of staff – the under master and the registrar – to join the committee. At the same time, the governors agreed to appoint a masters' salaries advisory body made up of four governors, three members of staff, the bursar and myself. This body did not have the power to set salaries but its recommendations to the governing body were seldom overturned. In the old days, Sir Henry had kept the masters' representatives waiting outside the room while the governers discussed whether to raise salaries and if so by how much.

Attempts to break down the barriers between the governors and the teaching staff were being made in many public schools at this time but, whereas other headmasters put their faith in social occasions, I believed that if a few influential members of staff worked alongside governors on a regular basis, they would gradually wean the common room from its traditional suspicion of the governing body. At the same time, the governors would discover that the members of staff were not militant trade unionists in middle-class clothing but professionals who understood perfectly well that their pay increases could not be allowed to price Westminster out of the market.

I was only partially successful. While a few governors and masters developed a mutual respect, the common room as a whole remained suspicious. The trouble was that the goodwill that was engendered by working together was swiftly dispelled when a bad decision or a clumsily-handled situation seemed to confirm what the common room had thought all along – that the governors were hopelessly out of touch. One of a headmaster's most difficult tasks is to explain the governors' decisions to the common room, particularly when he has argued against those decisions himself. I had to be loyal to the governors in public, but in private with friends I did not attempt to hide my impatience.

I disliked being caught in the middle between governors and staff. On one occasion, I arranged for a group of governors to discuss with housemasters the problems that arose as a result of having increasing numbers of boys and girls in the houses. We met in the Deanery under Edward Carpenter's chairmanship but instead of discussing ways of reducing pressure on housemasters, as the masters had expected, some of the governors launched into an attack on the housemasters' failure to impose good discipline. When the housemasters demanded to know what evidence there was, the governors could only answer unconvincingly that there was a general impression that discipline was slack.

The housemasters looked at me as though I had led them into a trap. When I tried to steer the discussion on to the size of houses, the more hawkish governors refused to be diverted and neither Edward nor I could stop them destroying in one hour whatever trust had been built up between the governing body and the common room in the previous year.

Most headmasters could tell similar stories about what are politely called 'misunderstandings' between governors and teaching staff. The pupils did not give a hoot who the governors were or what they did, but it mattered to the teaching staff, who found it frustrating that people with so little knowledge of running an independent school should have the final say in decisions that would make or mar the school's future.

The longer I remained a headmaster, the more critical I became of the role of the public school governing body but I could see no alternative. The headmaster had to be accountable to somebody. At Westminster at least the governors who were inclined to interfere in the running of the school were a small minority and they did not become a nuisance until the last years of my headmastership. On the strategic decisions, too, I had little cause for complaint because the governors eventually went along with all the major changes I proposed. But having to persuade them could be exasperating. What did they know about it? Of course Westminster needed to admit girls, to remove the religious restrictions on scholars, to increase numbers and spend millions on buying a new preparatory school and science department. To have to argue the case with governors who had no idea of the market in which Westminster had to operate was like being a chief executive with a board of directors who had no knowledge of the business.

My relations with governors were, therefore, mixed with impatience and anxiety. I was impatient that I could not get my own way quickly, yet anxious that I might lose the governors' confidence and be dismissed. That other headmasters experienced similar fears and frustrations was evident both from the way they spoke about their governors in unguarded moments, and from the frequency with which the Headmasters Conference found it necessary to intervene on their members' behalf. I never got to the stage of asking for help because the majority of Westminster's governors had neither the time nor the inclination to indulge in intrigue, but an unfortunate aspect of Westminster's constitution was that many of the more able governors came and went with their posts. The Master of Trinity College, Cambridge, left the governing body as soon as he left the Master's lodge but others with too little to occupy their minds went on until they themselves decided to retire. Eventually, Edward Carpenter persuaded the governors to discuss a compulsory retirement age; after much talk of the need for new blood and fresh ideas, they settled on the age of seventy-two and decided that even this rule should not apply to themselves.

In my relations with the governing body, I came to rely more and more on my friendship with Edward Carpenter. Westminster was one of the few public schools whose chairman of governors lived on the spot. The Deanery was a hundred yards from the headmaster's house and overlooked College Hall courtyard where the pupils gathered before their meals. If Edward Carpenter had been so minded he could have complained daily about the boys and girls who flung their books and cases at his door when they were late for lunch. But he was one of the few members of the Abbey community who seemed positively to enjoy living next door to six hundred adolescents. The other Abbey clergy and their wives found the proximity of so much youthful energy a strain on their some-what limited reserves of Christian charity. The morning stampede through the cloisters at one minute to nine was no respecter of persons, and clergy wives who ventured out risked being sent flying by boys who were late. Tea parties in secluded gardens were spoilt by cigarette ends thrown thoughtlessly from upper windows and the quiet contemplation of religious themes was rendered virtually impossible by the rowdiness of boarders on summer evenings.

The intermittent friction between school and Abbey did not dis-tract Edward and me from the important business of managing the relations between the school and the governing body. Two or three times a term, I walked round to the Deanery at about ten o'clock in the evening. We sat in Edward's book-lined study. He poured me a whisky and water. I lit a cigar. Together we tried to prevent the occurrence of events that might sour relations between the governors and the common room though, as the meeting with housemasters showed, we were not always successful. On other evenings, I wanted to talk about my own position vis-à-vis the governors. When Edward saw that I was anxious or frustrated, he would interpose a problem of his own. Typically, it concerned a memorial that people were pressing him to allow in the Abbey. One evening, when I arrived in a mood of uncertainty about my own future, he greeted me with the news that he needed my help over Poets' Corner. His decision to allow a memorial to the First World War poets had provoked unexpected controversy because no could agree which poets should be included. Some people were saying that Rupert Brooke and Julian Grenfell should be excluded because they regarded war as fun. It provoked me, as he knew it would, and I plunged into the argument with zest. The anxiety that had prompted my visit became less and less urgent as we debated the merits of the various candidates, so that by the time I was walking home by the light of the gas lamps in Dean's Yard, it had receded altogether.

The good fortune that has dogged me all my life played a part in Edward's appointment as Dean of Westminster and chairman of the governors. If there had been a different chairman, my relations with the governors might well have deteriorated long before they did. But Edward's appointment had depended on an unexpected change of government. When his predecessor, Eric Abbott, announced his retirement there was a Conservative government but, while soundings were being taken to find a successor, Heath called an election which returned Harold Wilson to power. Wilson told me some years later that there had been a clique with the Church, led by John Hewitt, who was responsible for advising the Prime Minister on ecclesiastical appointments, determined to block Edward's advancement because they regarded him as a radical and an outsider. I did not know that Wilson supported Edward and had reconciled myself to working with a chairman of governors who was a stranger and who might take a dim view of the school's eighteenth-century attitude towards religion.

I see the bursar this morning to discuss next year's fees and budget. During the discussion, Edward Carpenter telephones to say that 'the age of miracles has not passed'. I understand at once what he means and am overjoyed. But I replace the telephone and continue the discussion because the news is confidential until next week. It is marvellous and surprising because many influential Anglicans – including one of the governors – lobbied against him. To work with Edward as chairman of the governors is a pleasure and excitement I never thought to enjoy.

Edward became Dean in 1974 and retired in 1985, shortly before I left Westminster. We had our differences but not about the school. We worked together to defend Westminster's idiosyncratic tradition against those governors who wanted the boys and girls to be more like the pupils of a conventional public school. Edward was fond of quoting the epitaph of a seventeenth-century Cambridge mathematician, 'Where truth led, he dared to follow.' The words captured so exactly the spirit of Westminster's tradition that I suggested that we should adopt them as the school motto instead of the Victorian platitude – 'God giveth the increase'. Edward thought not. He knew better than I did that those governors who wanted to replace me with a more malleable headmaster needed no further encouragement. In such ways he protected me from myself as well as from my critics.

CHAPTER 10

Champion Turned Renegade

The man who had been educated at a minor public school and subsequently became an embittered critic of the public school system was a familiar figure in post-war Britain. What he resented so much was not the fact that public schools existed but that he had not attended a better one. In some respects, I conformed to this model. Even today, if I am asked where I was at school, I feel the need to add some explanation or apology, in case the questioner has not heard of Bishop's Stortford.

Such defensiveness must be incomprehensible to anyone who is unacquainted with the nuances of snobbery that used to be an essential part of the public school hierarchy and that exercised such a hypnotic spell over the English middle classes. Some vestiges of the snobbery remain – the major public schools still perform their traditional task of turning the sons of the *nouveaux riches* into the fathers of gentlemen – but parents nowadays are more interested in whether the school is any good than in whether its name casts a magic spell. I grew up in the old hierarchy and experienced its snubs and its magic. I was both attracted and repelled by its snobbery. I wanted to be accepted as an authentic public schoolboy but like a child who wants to destroy what he cannot have, I sometimes thought that the sooner the major public schools were abolished the better.

This response to the experiences of youth was gradually transformed into a rational critique of the role of the public schools.

The critique evolved over the years but the essence remained the same. I believed that, in a way that was peculiar to Britain, the public schools inhibited the development of well-educated society. As long as parents who could afford to do so automatically sent their children to public schools, the state schools that educated the majority of children would be seen as second best not only compared with the public schools but also – much more damagingly for the country – compared with the schools in other industrial societies. To put it simply, the public schools were holding Britain back. What had looked like a benign growth in the nineteenth century was beginning to look like a malignant one at the end of the twentieth.

What to do about it baffled me in the same way as it has baffled people of every political persuasion before and since. I believed in the public schools' right to exist in a free society just as strongly as other headmasters and I argued the case more often than any of them, but I did not know how to reconcile my critique of the public schools' role with my defence of their independence. It was a position that annoyed many people on both sides of the debate. I was accused of being two-faced, of biting the hand that fed me and of being liberal and left-wing.

'What's he like?' A woman asked me at a dinner party. 'Who?' I enquired. 'The headmaster, he's rather left-wing, I gather.' 'I am the headmaster.' 'Oh well, you should know then,' she continued unabashed.

I did know and I wasn't. I rejected all their labels. I saw nothing left-wing about recognizing the problem that the public schools posed while, at the same time, being prepared to defend their right to exist. To believe that the public schools presented no problem, or that they had no right to exist, seemed to me equally perverse.

People do not like complications. They want a simple answer to what they think is a simple question, 'Are you for public schools or against them?' Because I could not give an unqualified answer, I was regarded as unsound. On the face of it, therefore, I was not the best person to champion the public schools' cause in the media, yet that was the role I filled for several years.

It started in 1973. My brief flirtation with the press at Taunton encouraged me, once I had settled down at Westminster, to try my hand at journalism. I suggested to William Rees-Mogg, the editor of *The Times*, who lived round the corner and whose elder son went to school with Shamus and Jonathan, that I should write an article in defence of public schools. Thus began a career as a journalist that gave me an opportunity to publicize my view and gave my critics an opportunity to view me as a self-publicist. I *did* enjoy being in the public eye but the shallow celebrity that the media offered was a secondary motive. I wanted to influence the debate not only about public schools but also about the future of education. Imagining that I could influence the latter was perhaps another of those delusions of grandeur to which I was prone, but there were precedents for public school headmasters chancing their arm on public issues. The 'smiling, smirking' headmaster, wrote *John Bull* of Dr Arnold, should stop 'scribbling to papers when he should be attending to business.' Cyril Allington of Eton, a headmaster of a later generation, wrote so often in the newspapers, on so many different subjects, that 'his critics found his undoubted fondness for publicity unbecoming.' What was clear from the precedents was that any public school headmaster who tried to influence affairs outside his little kingdom would be attacked for courting publicity and neglecting his job.

The Times article prompted the BBC to invite me to take part in *The Sunday Debate*, a programme which took a controversial subject and allowed the protagonists and antagonists to argue it through to a conclusion on three consecutive Sunday evenings. That was in the days when the BBC was not afraid to allow an argument to run for longer than a few minutes. There was no studio audience, just a chairman – Robin Day – and two participants on either side. The subject was the future of the public schools. Norman St John Stevas, the Conservative Secretary of State for Education, and I put the case for the schools; Roy Hattersley, the Labour education spokesman, and Patrick Miller, a state schoolteacher, put the case against.

I consulted a number of colleagues in the Headmasters Conference but decided to stick to my own argument: the public schools *were* divisive and they *did* inhibit the improvement of state education but that did not constitute grounds for their abolition. I think St John Stevas would have liked something more uncompromising and robust. Roy Hattersley had come prepared to attack the public schools on the very grounds I was prepared to concede and found himself instead on the defensive in a debate about freedom. By being honest about my own ambivalence, I had outmanoeuvred the opposition. On the final programme, two independent assessors summed up decisively in my favour. Hattersley congratulated me. St John Stevas, who had found it difficult to get into the debate, left in a hurry.

The Sunday Debate launched me as the unlikely champion of the public schools. The irony was that the contradictions in my attitude had proved the best defence. For the next five years, whenever the abolitionists threw down the gauntlet, I was sent into the lists. In speeches, articles and pamphlets, I developed my ideas and arguments. The editor of the *Times Educational Supplement* invited me to contribute a regular fortnightly column, which I did for four years. The Headmasters Conference elected me chairman of its Political and Public Relations Committee and then, in 1977, chairman of the Conference itself. At forty-six, I was the youngest chairman for twenty years.

My frequent articles in the press, my appearances on television and my swift rise through the ranks of the Conference inspired envy. In the public school world, effortless celebrity was acceptable; anything that looked like self-advertisement was not. 'He abhors personal publicity', it was said of one of my critics, but in my experience the only thing most public school headmasters abhorred was that one of their rivals should receive more public attention than they did. The idea that they were shrinking violets who would die of embarrassment if their name appeared in the newspapers was ridiculous. Most of them wanted publicity for themselves and their schools but did not want to be seen trying to obtain it. What annoyed them was that I seemed to have cornered the market; because the media regarded me as the spokesman for independent schools, other headmasters' views were seldom sought.

I worried more about the reaction of the pupils. Some of the senior boys and girls did not like their school or their headmaster receiving too much exposure in the media. They were scornful of television as a medium for serious debate and dismissive of 'television personalities'. The editors of the school magazine could, and did, subject my newspaper articles to criticism, and when I took lunch in College Hall the scholars had no qualms about cross-questioning me on something that I had said or written. The pupils more than anyone else acted as a brake on any fantasies I may have had about becoming a public figure; the need to retain their respect ensured that being the spokesman for independent schools did not distract me from my job as their headmaster. Not that there was much chance of my being distracted. The everyday demands of school life were too absorbing, too full of unexpected crises, and of conflicts whose resolution could not be postponed. The defence of public schools was never more than a peripheral interest that I was happy to pursue when I had the time.

The teaching staff seldom commented. Either they were not interested or they thought it prudent to keep their views to themselves. The governors were happy as long as I was championing the public schools but, when my interventions in the educational debate became more controversial, their enthusiasm for having a well-known headmaster waned. There was another risk in being too close to the media: the publicity might not always be favourable. I accepted the risk. If I used the media to put across my views, I could not complain if the media sometimes paid me attention that I did not welcome. But I was also accepting the risk on behalf of the school and the family. The school did not suffer from the publicity I brought in – on the contrary – but my family did. Daphne and the children did not wish to be in the public eye; life in the headmaster's house was public enough without the intrusions of the press.

Roy Hattersley had stated that it was the Labour Party's 'serious intention initially to reduce and eventually to abolish private education in this country'. After *The Sunday Debate*, neither he nor the Labour Party put it in those terms again. One television programme had not changed their minds, but the public defeat of the Labour Party's arguments made the independent schools more confident and their enemies more cautious. The abolition of private education was not dropped from Labour Party policy until the 1980s, but from 1973 onwards the threat of abolition lacked credibility. When Labour returned to power in 1974, it turned its attention away from the public schools and concentrated on removing the government subsidies to the so-called direct grant schools, selective day schools that stood between the fully-independent public schools and the fully-funded state schools.

I was not sorry to see these subsidies disappear. In a competitive market, I saw no reason why some schools should receive taxpayers' money to keep down their fees. The government's job was to provide the best possible education for all children, not to offer financial inducements to some parents to opt out of state schools. I did not appreciate at the time that I would fall out with my colleagues in the Headmasters Conference over this issue and that it would help to accelerate my departure from Westminster.

Unable to prevent the ending of the direct grant, the independent schools spent the years 1974–1979 improving their image and creating a more unified structure to protect their interests. Although I played a central role in this strategy, I thought it was a mistake for the independent schools to be too much on the defensive. Our long-term survival did not really depend on the Labour Party but on public opinion, and public opinion would be more sympathetic if the schools took an active interest in mainstream education. Other headmasters did not agree, saying that it was not our job to tell politicians how to run the state sector of education. For years, public school headmasters had been actively discouraged from commenting on what was happening to education in the country as a whole.

This attitude made sense if the aim was to maintain the status quo – a flourishing independent sector alongside what would always be a second-class system of state schools. But I did not want to maintain the status quo. I still did not know how to reconcile the creation of first-class state schools with the continued existence of the public schools but I thought that the answer must lie in a radical change in central government's role in education. As things stood, central government did not have the power to improve the standards in state schools. Teachers could teach what they liked. The most idiotic ideas of the progressive educationalists could turn a school into an Alice in Wonderland world where no pupils ever failed and all pupils received prizes. No wonder that even the most dubious independent schools were able to fill their places with refugees from the state system.

With these thoughts, I set out to defy the convention that public school headmasters should stay out of the political minefield of state education. My year as chairman of the Headmasters Conference in 1977 coincided with what became known as the Great Debate in education, a series of public discussions up and down the country, inaugurated by the Prime Minister, James Callaghan, and carried through by his Secretary of State for Education, Shirley Williams. Callaghan was responding to widespread public disquiet about falling standards in state schools. If ever there was an opportunity for the public schools to make an impact on the wider education scene this was it.

At the beginning of the year, I wrote a long article for *The Times* arguing that unless there was greater central government control of education, particularly over what was taught in schools, we should never have an education system good enough to compete with other industrialized countries; and, in a television programme which was part of the Great Debate, I called on the government to impose a common-core curriculum on all schools, an idea that was immediately rejected on the same programme by Shirley Williams and by St John Stevas who was now the education spokesman in opposition.

A national curriculum was not a new idea – it had been operating in countries such as France and Japan for generations – but to advocate it in Britain in 1977 was to place oneself out on a limb. Neither public schools nor state schools liked the idea, all political parties rejected it and the press was almost uniformly hostile. I cannot have been the only person in the country who thought it a good idea but if there were others they kept remarkably quiet.

I discovered that being out on a limb was fun. So was being provocative. I got a kick out of reading in *The Times*, 'John Rae's outspokenness has antagonized not a few independent school heads.' There would have been no point in controversy for its own sake; it was a means to an end, a way of ensuring publicity for ideas I believed in. But unpopularity can be as intoxicating as popularity and just as deceptive. The more my idea of a national curriculum was dismissed as dangerous and fascist, the less inclined I was to think that anyone else's views were worth bothering with. I was falling for the most seductive of arguments – if everyone is against you, you must be right.

When the annual meeting of the Headmasters Conference came round in September, I used my chairman's address to return to the theme. 'I do not see how we are going to make the education system more responsive to the changing historical situation,' I told my colleagues, 'unless central government has more power to tell us, the teachers, what to do.' Though the headmasters applauded, they did not like it. For their chairman to advocate giving central government more power to dictate the curriculum must have seemed to many of them outrageous, particularly when a Labour government was in office.

Neither my fellow headmasters nor the governors of Westminster were comfortable with the increasingly eccentric line that I was taking in public. I wrote too much and not always about education; I advocated the abolition of the House of Lords as well as the ending of academic specialization in the sixth form, the reform of the trade unions as well as the introduction of the national curriculum. It would not have been surprising if my critics had muttered that I should stop 'scribbling to papers' when I should be 'attending to business'.

I was finally driven into the wilderness as far as my fellow headmasters were concerned over the Assisted Places Scheme. The name will mean nothing to most people. It was not a major educational reform but, for me, it was a test case: if the heads of independent schools supported the scheme they would demonstrate that they were more concerned with filling places in their own schools than with raising standards in the education system as a whole.

The origin of the scheme lay in the Labour Party's decision to end the subsidies to the direct grant schools. The heads of these schools lobbied the Conservative Party to restore the subsidy in some form when it returned to power. For those in favour of a two-tier education system, the strategy of these heads was correct: they wished to return to a situation in which they could offer places at their schools to promising children from poorer homes. Their leader, James Cobban, headmaster of Abingdon School, was a man of integrity and great energy who almost single-handedly persuaded the Conservatives to adopt the Assisted Places Scheme as party policy. I liked Cobban and though we disagreed absolutely about the scheme, it never affected our relationship.

The essence of the scheme was to provide taxpayers' money to send bright state schoolchildren to fee-paying schools. Parents who wanted to move their children from state schools, and whose children qualified academically, would apply for financial assistance and, if their income was low enough, their children would be given an assisted place at the independent school of the parents' choice.

It sounded harmless enough until you thought about the implications. One was that all state schools were equally bad, so that any parent who wanted to opt out was justified. But if it was true that all children in state schools were being starved of a good education, fundamental reforms were needed, not cosmetic gestures. You do not deal with a famine by sending a few lucky children to lunch at the Ritz. If, on the other hand, some children in the state schools were receiving a good education, there was no case for spending public money to move them. But the Scheme provided no check on whether the children needed to move. If I had been a state school headmaster, I should have been insulted by the implication that any independent school must be better than mine. It was well known at the time, as it is today, that in some parts of the country the state schools' academic results were better than those of the local independent schools.

None of these arguments found favour with my fellow headmasters. Though some had private doubts they kept them to themselves. I was the only one to speak out publicly against the scheme. I could understand the attitude of the heads of the former direct grant schools but not the silence of the others who knew the scheme was ill-conceived and that it would alienate us still further from those who worked in the state schools. I thought their silence was a betrayal. At a time when the country needed to raise the standard of education for all children, they were, by their silence, cynically endorsing a scheme that would cream off the best state school pupils to fill empty places in the independent schools. But, for most headmasters, political considerations were paramount. The Assisted Places Scheme was Conservative Party policy and the Conservatives were the public schools' natural allies.

I wrote and spoke against the scheme at every opportunity. The Labour Party was delighted. The Conservatives were not. St John Stevas described my attacks on the scheme as a 'distorted and partisan piece of polemic'. One of the few people from the independent school world who offered support was Sir Robert Birley, the former headmaster of Eton but he, too, was regarded as left-wing. (Birley's left-wing reputation had even less justification than mine; a portrait of Brahms on his wall had once been mistaken for Karl Marx.)

My disagreement with my colleagues on this issue came to a head at the Annual General Meeting in Cambridge in 1979. The chairman had arranged an open debate on the Assisted Places Scheme to clear the air and give the public school headmasters a chance to show that they were united in support of Tory education policy. If I attacked the scheme, I would be accused of rocking the boat; if I did not, I would be accused of trimming my sails to the prevailing wind. I decided to be a rocker not a trimmer. At one point, I was shouted down, an unusual experience when addressing public school headmasters. The trouble was that they had had enough; enough of my opposition to the scheme and enough of my hogging of the limelight. In their eyes, the erstwhile defender of the public schools had become a renegade.

No longer entirely at ease in formal gatherings of public school headmasters, though retaining the friendships I had made with individuals, I concentrated on trying to ensure that the Westminster governors did not decide to join the Assisted Places Scheme. Sooner or later it was bound to be raised, if for no other reason than because one or two governors would not be sorry to put me in a difficult position. But, when it was raised in the summer of 1980, Lord Trend and Lord Carr (a former Conservative Home Secretary) spoke with such authority against having anything to do with the Scheme, neither Edward nor I had to contribute to the debate. For the time being, this potentially dangerous topic was off the governing body's agenda.

Perhaps I should have let matters rest there. I had conducted a long campaign against the scheme but I had failed to stop it being introduced or to dissuade other headmasters from giving it their support. There was both stubbornness and arrogance in my decision to continue my opposition. As had been the case with the national curriculum, the strength of the hostility I aroused did nothing to undermine my conviction that I was right. Stubborn and arrogant

I may have been; 'inconsistent' and 'insincere' – two epithets used by my critics – I was not. Much as I enjoyed provoking people, it would have been stupid to go on attacking what was now government policy unless I believed in my arguments. The charge of inconsistency always annoyed me. When it came to the defence of the public schools, I saw eye to eye with the Tories; when it came to opposition to the Assisted Places Scheme, I was content to be identified with the socialists. In *The Sunday Debate*, I spoke alongside St John Stevas; in a Cambridge Union debate on the Assisted Places Scheme, I spoke alongside Neil Kinnock. I was not prepared to suppress my doubts about the scheme in order to appear politically consistent.

Yet all the time I was defending the public schools, I was aware of my ambivalence towards them. I would have fought hard to defend Westminster's freedom, but when the boys and girls from the local state schools paid a visit and I watched the state and the public school pupils trying to make contact with one another – both groups as wary as if they were from different countries – I could not help thinking that the public schools did not merely reflect the divisions in our society, as I had so often argued in debate, but were instrumental in keeping those divisions alive. If the children of the duke and the dustman attended the same school, no differences of wealth or ancestry could make them treat one another as foreigners.

My ambivalence was never more evident than in my decision to apply for the headmastership of Eton. When Michael McCrum announced in 1979 that he was going to retire, the controversy over the Assisted Places Scheme was at its height. There was not the remotest chance that the Fellows – Eton's governing body – would risk appointing someone who had identified himself with the Labour Party and who had a knack of attracting publicity, which was the last thing Eton needed. But I went ahead with my application all the same. I was powerfully attracted by those very qualities – the grandeur, the wealth, the patrician manners and the aristocratic traditions – that made Eton the most divisive public school of all. One newspaper predicted that if I was appointed I would 'shake Eton to its roots' but I was far too ambivalent to be a radical reformer. My attempts to reform Eton would have been half-hearted and messy. Fortunately, for Eton and myself, I was not given the opportunity.

In 1980, I was forty-nine and had been headmaster of Westminster for ten years. I did not want to leave but neither did I want to stay until the retiring age of sixty-two. There were no other schools apart from Eton that I wanted to be headmaster of, even if they would have me. Nor was there any other job I was qualified to do. Public school headmasters are singularly ill-equipped to move into other types of employment; it is like trying to find a job for a deposed dictator. There were times when I envied the Roman Catholic headmasters – Benedictines and Jesuits – who were headmasters one day and humble parish priests the next. But if you have not taken vows of poverty, chastity and obedience, your freedom to relinquish power is restricted by the need to provide for your family and to secure your pension.

So I put thoughts of looking for another job out of my mind. I was lucky to be at Westminster. With its tradition of worldliness and non-conformity, it was probably the only public school in which I would ever feel at home.

CHAPTER 11

Hazards for the Headmaster's Family

When we moved to Westminster, Siobhan, the oldest of our six children, was thirteen. My predecessor had had no children. His predecessor had left because the headmaster's house was unsuitable for a young family. Space was not the problem: there were nine bedrooms and three bathrooms. The problem was lack of privacy. There was no other headmaster's house I had ever seen where the staff common room was on the ground floor and where pupils and teachers looking for the headmaster were likely to appear unexpectedly in the bedroom corridor. Seeing a naked stranger wrapped in a towel emerge from the spare bedroom, Daphne challenged him; he was the fencing 'professor' who had used the room for changing for many years and had not thought to ask whether he could continue to do so. Since he spoke little English (he had escaped from Hungary at the time of the 1956 uprising) his attempts to explain himself to the headmaster's wife were not immediately successful.

Number seventeen, Dean's Yard, was an open house in another sense. The front door was never locked during the day, allowing some of the cranks, tramps and thieves who were attracted to the Abbey precincts to find their way into the hall and up the stairs. Daphne was rather adept at apprehending thieves but when she handed them over to me, I let them slip. 'Would you mind waiting in here for a moment?' I asked one thief who wore an all too obvious red wig like a circus clown; I had a visiting speaker in the drawing room and a boy in the study who had been sent to me for telling the director of music to 'Sod off!' Thieves were a low priority.

There was something about this way of living that appealed to me. It must have been the element of French farce. And if, in the juggling of visitors and trespassers, the occasional thief went missing, he was no great loss. But, to the family, the lack of privacy was less appealing. It was not so much the danger of strangers as the feeling that there was nowhere to escape to. The children tried a variety of tactics to protect their privacy including a notice which read: 'No one but family beyond this point – private property', but the stream of visitors up and down the stairs to my study meant that only late at night could the family have the house to themselves, and even then, if I was out, they had to field the angry and abusive telephone calls that sometimes followed an expulsion.

Living in a fine Regency house in a cathedral close in the centre of London was some compensation for the lack of privacy. Though Daphne was never entirely at ease in the city, the children became wholeheartedly Londoners. When they were young, the Abbey and its precincts were their playground, and as they grew older they were more at home on the streets of the capital than they would have been in the countryside. I think they enjoyed being at the centre of things as much as I did. It was fun to walk out of your front door to join the crowd on some great occasion or just to stroll across the parks to Piccadilly.

It was not living in the heart of London that caused problems for the children but having a headmaster for a father. They were always identified as the headmaster's children. They had to run the gauntlet of curious or hostile eyes. The girls in particular disliked having to push their way through a crowded outer hall where boys were lobbying members of staff and an inner hall where assorted rogues were waiting to see me. It was difficult, too, for them to come to terms with the fact that although I was at home, I so seldom had time for them. I did not like their having to knock on the study door and say, 'I know you're busy, Daddy . . .' as though they were members of staff seeking an audience, but I could not prevent the pressure of work coming between me and the family. On three or four evenings a week, I was out, fulfilling speaking engagements, dining with parents, attending school functions or just taking a disgruntled colleague to the pub. One evening, when Daphne was away, I noted this exchange with Shamus who was then eleven.

'Are you going out, Daddy?'
'No.'
'At least we've got a father this evening.'

After dealing with other people's children all day it was sometimes a struggle to give our own the time and attention they needed. Over supper it was tempting to let Alyce's elaborate tale of why Miss So-and-So was a useless teacher go in one ear and out the other; or to leave Daphne to answer when Emily wanted to know why she had to be home by eleven. Complaints about teachers and questioning of the rules had been the bread and butter of my day. I would have been glad of a change of problem but, even so, I found it difficult to slough off the authoritarian manner. I was so accustomed to interrupting what other people said, and so unaccustomed to being contradicted, that my children sometimes had difficulty making themselves heard. It is often said that a headmaster's children bring him down to earth, that when he crosses the threshold between school and home he is no longer allowed the delusions of grandeur that have sustained him during the day. This may be true but for the children it can be a tricky, even hazardous operation, like coaxing an elephant back into its cage: the beast may look harmless enough but its mood is uncertain. There were times when the irritation I had suppressed during the day in order to preserve the image of the calm headmaster, could be triggered at home by a child's innocent remark. It did not happen often but, when it did, the emotion fed upon itself; I was angry because I was angry, annoyed with myself for losing my temper with my children when I should have lost it with a member of staff.

Being the headmaster's children also had advantages. Not only did they live in interesting surroundings, they met interesting people. But the real advantage, I suspect, was having a father who had seen many young people safely on the journey to adulthood. So that when Penelope slammed the door and said she was leaving, or Emily walked out of her boarding-school and caught the next train to London, or Jonathan took pot shots with his air gun at one of the Westminster housemasters, I did not think there was much cause for concern because I knew that in adolescence it was the arrival not the journey that mattered.

I tried to capture our children's childhood, and perhaps to tell them in a roundabout way how much I loved them, by writing stories in which they appeared. Over a period of six years, I wrote a series of children's books in which they took it in turn to play the principal character. The first, published in 1974, was called *The Golden Crucifix* and told the story of Siobhan's part in the Gunpowder Plot; the last, a ghost story about Shamus and Jonathan, called *The Third Twin*, was published in 1980. I wrote the books in the holidays but worked out the plots at odd moments during the term, such as Abbey matins, which I attended with the scholars on one Sunday in each month; the sermon was seldom worth listening to, so I took the opportunity to develop the plot while keeping an eye on the scholars whose bored or enigmatic expressions no doubt hid more exotic flights of fancy.

When Siobhan, Penelope and Emily came to Westminster in the sixth form (Alyce was happy remaining in her girls' school), they felt even more acutely than most pupils the need to be accepted by their peers, who not unnaturally wondered how much the girls might pass on to their father. 'We can't talk in front of Penelope,' they would say, until a few illicit visits to the pub had earned their trust. 'We had to be bad to be accepted,' Siobhan told me some years later, 'we couldn't grass if we were involved.'

Their peccadillos were bound to come my way. Siobhan was caught in a pub with four boys and although the offence would normally have been dealt with by the housemaster, perhaps because Siobhan was amongst them, they were all sent to me. I gave them a standard warning for a first offence but Siobhan remembers that I asked her to stay behind and said, 'For God's sake, if you're going to drink, drink far enough away so you don't get caught.'

When our daughters had these minor brushes with the school rules, I was relieved rather than angry; they and I both benefited from the discovery that the headmaster's children were not paragons of virtue. There was also something to be said for the girls being able to rebel against their father without their rebellion being too personal. But their desire to be seen as uninhibited members of the school could produce embarrassing moments. When the curtain went up on the house play, there was Siobhan sitting on stage in a short skirt and fishnet stockings, smoking a cigarette. The play was *Zigger Zagger*. Daphne soon walked out, as she was in the habit of doing if she disapproved of the language or content of a play, but that only enhanced Siobhan's standing with her peers. On the other hand, teaching our own children presented no problems. I taught all three daughters A-level History; I treated them like any other pupils and they treated me like any other teacher.

It was less easy for the other teachers to be sure how to treat the headmaster's children. Emily threw her pen at one man who made a crack about the headmaster. Other masters were ingratiating. The girls came to like and respect a number of teachers. Their respect for Jim Cogan was predictable because he accepted them from the start as pupils in their own right (confirming my view that he was a rare phenomenon – a school master with no trace of insecurity), but I was surprised to find how loyal they were to masters I regarded as over the hill. One man, in particular, I thought had lost all interest in his subject but Siobhan would not have a word said against him, so much so that I was forced to acknowledge that I had been too dismissive of the man because he so obviously disliked the changes I had made and did not hide his preference for the *ancien régime*.

While they were in the school, Siobhan, Penelope and Emily were selective in what they mentioned at home; they never grassed on their contemporaries though they had no hesitation in talking about the boys they liked, who always seemed to be those who were 'misunderstood by their housemaster'. If they found the rogues more attractive than the 'creeps', that was normal. Sometimes they invited the rogues back to our house and I would come across them, doing their best to look sheepish as they padded like wolves along the bedroom corridor. Or I would sink into an armchair in the half light to watch the television news and become aware of a boy or two sitting on the sofa with the girls. As parents do, Daphne and I tried to monitor the relationships that developed but, because the boys were pupils, I did not take the relationships seriously. How wrong I was became clear when two of our daughters married former Westminster boys who had been their contemporaries.

There were times when I had to admire the *sang froid* of our daughters' boyfriends. One of them was under suspicion of being involved in drugs and would be expelled if the substance I had sent to the Home Office Dangerous Drugs Inspectorate turned out to be cannabis. The young man appeared at a tea party for confirmation candidates in our drawing room. Watching him chatting up the Bishop and making himself useful, there was no way of telling whether he knew what the answer from the Home Office would be. He came over to offer me a cucumber sandwich and to ask whether it was all right for him to take our daughter to the cinema at the weekend. He was checking up on whether I had heard and reminding me that a member of the family had an interest in the outcome. Was this coolness in the face of danger another of those benefits of a Westminster education that did not appear in the prospectus?

For the three children who did not come to Westminster – Alyce, Shamus and Jonathan – number seventeen Dean's Yard was home and nothing else, and they probably resented more than their sisters the way in which the life of the school invaded every corner of the building. It was partly for this reason that we decided to send Shamus and Jonathan to boarding-school. Daphne had become a Roman Catholic in 1976 and we chose to send the boys to Downside, a Benedictine school in the West Country.

After the masters meeting to launch the term, I leave by train for the West Country. Daphne has driven Shamus and Jonathan to Downside early to buy school uniform and now I catch up with them in time for the headmaster's talk to new boys and their parents. Shamus and Jonathan look a little apprehensive; they have never been away from home before. It is a bitterly cold day with snow blowing about in the school yard, too hectic to settle. Tea with other parents, a few last words, and then Daphne and I depart, leaving Shamus and Jonathan playing table tennis together in a rather bleak day room. Why, I ask myself, do the British do this to their children?

Even if Westminster had been the right school for Shamus and Jonathan, I would not have sent them there. It was relatively easy for the girls at sixteen to handle the problems of being the headmaster's children; it would have been much more difficult for the twins to do so at thirteen. I knew of too many cases where the headmaster's sons had been miserable at their father's school. Nevertheless, we sent our sons to boarding-school with reluctance. Perhaps they sensed our lack of enthusiasm. After a few terms, Shamus had had enough; as Emily had done before him, he walked out and caught the train to London. Jonathan followed shortly after because he wanted to be with his brother.

We were not embarrassed about our children's propensity for walking out of boarding-school; Daphne and I had done the same. Nor did we blame the schools or try to persuade our children to return. That was not because we were careless of our children's education but because we had faith that they would come good in their own time and that it was unnecessary, therefore, to worry overmuch about setbacks along the way. My knowledge of how the system worked helped. So did my experience of other boys and girls who had only begun to realize their potential after they had left school. So did my father's refusal to accept that just because I failed the equivalent of A level I should abandon all thought of university. I was profoundly sceptical of the English approach to education, which rejected children if they did not reach a certain standard at a prescribed age. I took it for granted that some of our children would fall at early hurdles and then develop their talents later, because that was in their genes, and I was determined that no teacher was going to write our children off by labelling them 'unfit for further education'. Two of our children were described as 'backward' at the age of eight. When they both obtained their first degrees at university, Daphne wanted to go and see the teacher and tell her just how wrong she had been. I dissuaded her because I recalled cases in which Westminster, too, had badly underestimated the potential of its pupils. But my experience of our own children's education made me realize how important it was to impress upon pupils and their parents that the judgement of schools and teachers should not be regarded as immutable truth. The decision of the education system is never final.

Daphne belonged to a generation of women whose careers were profoundly affected by the low expectations of their teachers. Unless they were lucky in their parents or their school, women of that generation were assumed to have reached their academic ceiling roughly at O level, or what is now GCSE. Our father never doubted that Angus and I should go to university and that our sisters, Bobby and Susan, should not, but, as far as I am aware, there was no evidence for making that distinction.

For the first twenty years of married life, Daphne was devoted to bringing up six children. By 1976, the youngest, Shamus and Jonathan, were ten and would probably be going away to boarding-school in a few years. Whether Daphne would be willing to settle for just being a headmaster's wife was always doubtful.

Tom Brown's Schooldays, the best known of all school stories, was not dedicated to Thomas Hughes's headmaster, Dr Arnold, as might have been expected, but to the headmaster's wife. 'To Mrs Arnold,' Hughes wrote, 'this book is (without her permission) dedicated by the author who owes more than he can ever acknowledge or forget to her and hers.' The 'hers' presumably includes the headmaster but he is something of an afterthought. It is usually the other way around.

The role of a headmaster's wife in an English public school is difficult to define. Since her husband is a public figure, she is expected to accompany him on numerous social occasions and to be able to entertain with equal facility the shyest new boy and the most self-important distinguished guest. Mrs Arnold regularly had the boys to tea, as headmaster's wives still do, but few women today would be satisfied with a role that falls somewhere between a housekeeper and a hostess. It is not unknown for the headmaster's wife to pursue her own career but it is still frowned upon by some governing bodies who, while they may not know exactly what the headmaster's wife's role should be, are sure that it should be defined by the needs of the school.

The ill-defined role is accompanied by a sense of not belonging. Her home is not her own. Her husband is not her own; he is public property. She probably sees more of him than most wives do but she has less of his attention. In term time, the school is his mistress and he visits her at all hours; in the holiday, she is seldom off his mind.

For Daphne, the common problems of being a headmaster's wife were exacerbated by being married to someone of my temperament. I cannot make out whether I was born so reticent and wary of relationships, or whether that side of my nature was simply re-enforced again and again by circumstances of childhood, the need to survive at boarding-school and the demands of headmastering. Whichever it was, I developed such a defensive manner that, even with my own family, I was careful not to give too much away.

Our marriage broke down because we found it increasingly difficult to live with one another. The tension between our private and public lives may have accelerated the process but it was not to blame. As the children grew up, the precarious nature of our relationship was exposed. Rather than face up to the painful and possibly hopeless task of recreating that relationship, I became increasingly preoccupied with surviving and succeeding in my job, a familiar male alibi for failing sexual and emotional interest. Daphne was too energetic and too intelligent to be satisfied with a life made up of two ill-defined and largely unappreciated supporting roles.

We separated in 1976. Our relationship had become so strained that a break was welcome to us both. It was not welcome to the children; Daphne was a good mother and they missed her. Shamus and Jonathan were only ten but it was the girls in their teens who seemed to be more disorientated by the separation. It is easy, now, to take a detached view because the break in the marriage turned out to be a blessing, a breathing space that Daphne and I both needed, but we did not know and will probably never know what effect it had on the children. Westminster parents who were separating would tell me that it was all very amicable and that their son or daughter would not be adversely affected but I doubt whether there is any other subject on which parents are more likely to deceive themselves.

A headmaster separated from his wife would have been regarded as scandalous by the governors of a country boarding-school but Westminster's governors took a characteristically worldly view. One or two of the clerics were jumpy when they were telephoned by a tabloid newspaper, and one or two of my critics thought they saw an opportunity to ease me out, but Edward Carpenter and Burke Trend kept their colleagues steady. They also dictated the official line. 'The headmaster and his wife are living apart but the headmaster is continuing at Westminster with the full support of the governing body.' One gossip-columnist wrote a piece on 'Where is the headmaster's wife?' making much of the Abbey connection and of the fact that the Bishop of London was a prominent former pupil, but for the most part the separation was a matter for private adjustment not public comment.

Gradually, over a period of several months, Daphne and I tried to put the marriage together again. The governors were patient but they wanted us to make a decision about our future one way or the other. When Daphne eventually returned for good, the school community treated her as though nothing had happened, but one or two members of the Abbey community declined to talk to her. What worried Daphne was not the smallmindedness of some of our neighbours but the need to find a new direction in her life. As a girl, she had wanted to be a doctor but her ambition had been thwarted by a limitation typical of girls' schools at that time: there was no science teaching other than a ramble through the more ladylike aspects of biology. Without qualifications there was no chance of entry to medical school. It was too late now to become a doctor but not too late to fulfil her childhood ambition to work with the sick and suffering.

She had become a Roman Catholic shortly after her return, and the new Archbishop of Westminster, Father Basil Hume, encouraged her to do a postgraduate diploma of pastoral theology with the Jesuits' Heythrop College in the University of London. It was not medicine but it paved the way for a new departure in her life. For two years, she worked part-time at a home for the terminally ill and dying, but part-time work was not enough. She had been born in the East and decided to return. In 1979, she wrote to the Sisters of Charity in Calcutta but received no reply. Mother Theresa was not concerned with correspondence; if people really wanted to work with the sisters they would come. So Daphne went to Heathrow airport and got on a plane to India.

Over the next seven years, she made several trips to India to work, first with the Sisters of Charity in Calcutta and then in a leprosy village in north Bihar near the Nepalese border. I admired, above all, her refusal to settle for a life of coffee mornings and playing at charity. In Calcutta, she helped to save life and to ease its passing, collecting unwanted babies from the abortion clinics and caring for the dying; in North Bihar, she dressed the sores of the leprosy patients in the makeshift hospital. The family adjusted without difficulty to her comings and goings but other people were uncertain how to react to this headmaster's wife who had left her husband and then come back again, who had become a Roman Catholic while her husband was head of an Anglican school, and who had taken off for India to immerse herself in death, leprosy and abortion. I fancy other headmasters' wives reacted with feelings of envy. How had Daphne Rae managed to get away with it?

Daphne got away with it because Westminster was relaxed about individuals who defied convention and because she was determined to do something with her life in addition to bringing up a large family. Many other wives and mothers have dreamed of doing the same but have lacked the opportunity or the courage and have made a virtue of necessity and stayed at home. Commuting between India and Westminster raised some eyebrows, nevertheless. There were, the residents of Dean's Yard were prepared to acknowledge, good biblical precedents for working with the poor and the lepers, but rescuing babies from abortion clinics was a little distasteful, even ostentatious.

Daphne made matters worse. She enjoyed shocking people with gruesome details. Unlike me, she had never developed the art of understatement. She let people know exactly what she thought. When a parent arrived early for an evening appointment and asked if he might have a whisky, she lectured him on the evils of drink. When she thought a play unsuitable she walked out. She responded with the same directness to dinner guests who asked her what she did in India. Yes, it was true that the aborted babies she could not rescue because they were too small to survive were flung in the dustbin and removed with the rest of the rubbish. The listeners found it difficult to process this piece of information. They were usually the sort of people – liberal, well-meaning, Anglican – who wanted to believe that the cruelties of the developing world could all be blamed on primitive ignorance or colonial oppression and did not know in which category the contents of those Calcutta dustbins should be placed.

One Easter holidays, Daphne persuaded me to accompany her to the leper village at Sunderpore in north Bihar. By way of preparation I read Shiva Naipaul's *Beyond the Dragon's Mouth*, in which he writes that Bihar is 'notorious for its squalor, its backwardness, its gross corruptions. It has become a byword for all that is most hopeless and terrible about the Indian condition: the subcontinent's heart of darkness ... typically, it was Bihar which caused a furore in the New Delhi Parliament when news broke that the police, as a matter of course, had been blinding scores of common criminals in their custody.'

Even if I had not read that passage, I should have found Bihar, with its hot, featureless landscape, a godforsaken place. Leprosy was endemic. So was violence. So was smuggling. Sunderpore straddled the border between India and Nepal and at night, smugglers with contraband on their heads moved silently through the village, knowing that the police would not enter the area where the lepers lived.

Daphne and I lived in a hut made of dried mud and cow-dung. The village day began at 4.30 a.m. because at 10 a.m. heat of the sun made almost any activity unbearable. In the early morning, Daphne went off to the hospital and I went to the school. The headmaster, Mr Rahindra, had been a deputy headmaster in another part of India and had lost his job when he had been unable to conceal any longer the fact that he had leprosy. Since that time, the disease had progressed. The ends of his fingers were missing, though he could hold a piece of chalk in the polished stumps and write on the blackboard. His features had also been deformed, the nose seeming to have caved in upon itself giving the face a curiously lion-like appearance. But, for all his deformities, he was a man of great dignity and *gravitas* whose firm voice and upright bearing signalled to the children that he expected from them the highest standards of behaviour.

When I arrived at the school on the first morning, he raised both arms to greet me and, fearing that he was going to embrace me, I held back. He smiled broadly. 'Welcome, headmaster,' he said.

Better to show your repulsion on first encountering the disease, I decided later, or your relationship with the leper starts with an act of deception. Not to be repulsed is unnatural. When the leper sees you overcome your repulsion, he can trust your feelings. But my ever-present hypochondria was not really susceptible to such neat rationalizations. Sunderpore was a hypochondriac's nightmare. Father Christdas, the Indian priest who ran the village, assured me that it was virtually impossible for me to contract leprosy; most of the world's population was immune. Such assurances bring no comfort to the hypochondriac because he is convinced that he is going to be the exception.

So, for several days, I made a point of keeping my distance from everyone in the village. As people came towards me I checked their feet to see whether the toes were missing. When I visited the hospital, I stuck to the middle aisle between the beds. One morning I spent in the out-patients' clinic only played on my worst fears; once I had learnt that the tell-tale sign on the skin was a small red or pale patch in which the feeling was dead, I made a daily check, as though the symptoms of leprosy could appear overnight.

The school was a long, low building with a bamboo frame, mud-packed walls and a grass roof. It was divided into five classrooms with small wooden desks. Each child had a metal box in which to carry exercise books and pencils. Mr Rahindra had written to Daphne to ask her to bring some pens for the children and we had arranged for these to be a gift from the preparatory school at Westminster. Unwisely, I had not checked the contents of the parcel. When Mr Rahindra distributed the pens, the children found that most of them did not write. The little rich boys had not donated new pens; they had taken the opportunity to dump their old ones.

Mr Rahindra introduced me to the boys and girls in the top group. He was not sure of their ages; between eleven and thirteen, perhaps. Until two years ago they had been begging on the streets of Raxaul, the nearby town. They did not have leprosy, and with any luck would never develop the disease, but in most cases both parents were lepers. When Father Christdas came to Sunderpore, he collected the children from the streets and started the school. The first aim was to teach literacy and numeracy so that lepers' children would not be cheated in the local market. Mr Rahindra told me that now the children in the top group were literate in Hindi and English. Perhaps I would like to teach them the finer points of English grammar.

So began for me a lesson in motivation. The children started work at dawn, took a long break in the heat of the day and were still demanding to be taught at 7.30 in the evening. Their drive was astonishing, as was their seemingly endless enthusiasm. They would not depart until I had set them their homework and then off they would go in the darkness carrying their metal boxes, to a hut where Mother without fingers was preparing the meal and Father, his hideous face wrapped in a white cloth, sat in the corner like an extra in a Hollywood biblical epic. I did not know when they did their homework or by what flickering firelight they identified the parts of speech in the sentences I had given them, but they never failed to do it and seldom failed to get it right. And this was at a time when progressive educationalists in Britain were arguing that children should not be given homework because it put those from working-class homes at a disadvantage.

Mr Rahindra's pupils soon exhausted my supply of English grammar. One boy in particular was always a step ahead of me, correcting my mistakes, suggesting new avenues of enquiry, asking the sort of awkward questions I associated with Westminster scholars. His name was Manjur Aman. Both his mother and father had been badly affected by leprosy but he was as bright as a button, too bright sometimes for my liking. Nothing could distract him from his relentless pursuit of accuracy, not even the mosquitoes, not even the skeletal, dust-coloured cats that turned up to my evening classes and 'meowed' so exactly like a human, I thought a boy in the back row was trying to wind me up.

'I think that's enough for today,' I said, amid protests.

I spoke to the headmaster about Manjur. What did a boy like that do at the age of thirteen when he had outgrown the village school? Mr Rahindra was not sure. The religious orders ran boarding-schools for the children of lepers but he was not keen. 'Institutional schools make children psychologically defective,' he told me. He hoped that Manjur and the other children would be allowed to attend the secondary school in Raxaul despite the hostility of the local people.

On our last evening in Sunderpore, there was a celebration of Father Christdas's birthday which mingled unselfconsciously the elements of a Hindu festival and a Catholic mass. In the moonlight, those with leprosy and those without sat together on the ground outside the hospital. At the end of the 'service', the schoolchildren, conducted by the headmaster, sang 'We shall overcome' in English. Feeling the emotion rise, I forced myself to take a detached view. I did not think they would overcome. One or two might escape to secondary school in Raxaul but what then? Where in this godforsaken place was all their English grammar leading?

Sitting in the aeroplane at Delhi airport, waiting to taxi to the runway, I suddenly burst into tears. What finally broke the well-trained British reserve was not the thought of the leprosy and the poverty of Sunderpore. It was just that Mr Rahindra and his children had such high hopes.

India gave Daphne a point of focus outside the family and the school. While bringing up six children, her field of vision had been necessarily restricted. The time spent in Calcutta and Sunderpore did not lessen her interest in Westminster. It had the opposite effect: because the ill-defined duties of a headmaster's wife were no longer the only alternative to family matters, she embraced them with enthusiasm. India helped our relationship too, not straightaway, and not without times when it seemed that our marriage would fail again. But India gave Daphne a story of her own; she was no longer just the wife of the headmaster of Westminster and that was a better basis for building a relationship that would survive when the children had gone. India also helped Daphne to find her own voice. She wrote a book about her experience in Calcutta, illustrated with her own photographs, which was published in 1979. Encouraged by its success, she started on a second book which she proposed to call *A World Apart*. It would be partly autobiographical and partly about public schools.

The visit to the leper village in Sunderpore was one of a number of experiences in the early 1980s that disorientated me (the brief involvement in *The Killing Fields* was another) and that, almost without my being aware, weakened at long last the cords that held me to the public school world. When the time came to leave Westminster, I found that the cords were already broken.

CHAPTER 12

Fighting Retreat

I started my second decade as headmaster of Westminster eager to demonstrate that I had not run out of steam. But ten years is a long time and at the beginning of each school year I looked forward to some aspects of the job more than others. It was impossible to be tired of the pupils because they were always changing, collectively and individually, and each new generation of fifteen and sixteen-year-olds managed to find fresh variations on familiar themes. The annual junior school expeditions invariably provided an opportunity for the urban adolescents to outwit authority. Required to compete in a long cross-country hike, two Dodgers slipped into a remote telephone box and ordered a taxi, so that when the master in charge strode into the village that marked the finish, under the impression that he had won, he saw them sitting in the sun on a bench outside the pub. He demanded to know how they had arrived before him. 'We hired a taxi, sir,' was the reply.

I relished these stories not because I lacked respect for the master – on the contrary, he was a friend and an ally – but because the clash between the best intentions of teachers and the base cunning of adolescents seemed to me a true expression of what schools were about.

I looked forward, also, to working with those members of staff who shared my idea of what sort of school Westminster should be. After a long summer holiday, it was a pleasure to see them again and to debate with renewed optimism how we were going to maintain

Westminster's competitive edge and keep at bay those governors and masters who wanted Westminster to be a more conventional public school.

These were the themes that preoccupied me and my closest colleagues during the last period of my headmastership. Though the changes of the early years had strengthened Westminster's competitive position, the underlying problems had not gone away. The school was still short of space. The swing from boarding to day was still forcing up the total numbers. Illegal drugs were still accessible for those boys and girls who wished to indulge. While we continued to wrestle with these problems, we did not believe that solving them would guarantee Westminster's market. What made Westminster's brand of education distinctive was the combination of high academic standards with an unusual tolerance of individuality and non-conformity.

The academic results in the early 1980s were better than ever now that the practice of concentrating on the brightest pupils had been abandoned. What the old guard had dismissed as 'the Gadarene rush to A levels' had paid off. Comparing notes with our competitors, I found that only Eton, Winchester and St Paul's were in the same league. But Westminster's other selling-point was more difficult to pin down. You could not measure the degree to which non-conformity was tolerated and encouraged. Some pupils would have denied that it was tolerated at all. To them, tolerance of non-conformity meant freedom to do what they wished. But license kills non-conformity as quickly as repression. The secret, as any parent or head teacher knows, is to allow enough freedom for individuality to flourish but not enough for it to be spoilt. What gave Westminster's approach to the problem its characteristic flavour was that for centuries non-conformity had been regarded as a virtue. Whereas, in most public schools, the pupils who did not conform had been regarded as odd, even subversive, at Westminster, learning not to conform had always seemed to be the point of the exercise. When Philip Henry, a seventeenth-century Westminster pupil, told his headmaster 'you taught me those things that hindered me from conforming', he was expressing what, for me, was the essence of the Westminster tradition.

The tradition had not made Westminster a gentle place. Bullying, flogging and brutality had been part of Westminster's history just as much as tolerance and non-conformity. The scholars' dormitory had been as harsh a preparation for manhood as any in a civilized country. 'Were it not for the dormitory at Westminster and the quarter deck of a man of war,' one eighteenth-century admiral claimed, 'we should be a nation of macaronis.' By the 1980s, though Westminster was not quite the gentle and civilized place it appeared on the surface, the brutality had gone and the respect for non-conformity remained.

It was a tradition I cherished as much as I could, though it had its down side. Posing as a non-conformist is an adolescent pastime and Westminster had more than its share of posers. It had a few macaronis too, modern equivalents of those insolent eighteenth-century fops who belonged to the Macaroni Club. The trouble with the posers and the macaronis was that they caught the eye and gave some governors and members of staff an excuse to attack the way the school was being run. I did not much like the posers and the macaronis either, but I reckoned they were a price we had to pay for creating the conditions in which non-conformity would flourish. When I urged pupils to question everything, I hoped they would become independent-minded adults. The fact that some of them would be a pain in the neck as adolescents did not seem to me a matter of great concern.

Those governors and members of staff who took a different view were not an organized opposition and I did not worry about them as long as I had the support of the majority. But, in 1983, that support was suddenly and unexpectedly put in doubt.

The governors gave me a sabbatical term in the spring which I spent in Thailand, where David Puttnam was setting up *The Killing Fields*, and in New York, where I was a visiting teacher at Trinity School in Manhattan. I returned to Westminster refreshed. At the start of the summer term, Daphne and I gave a party for former Harrow boys we had known well to mark the publication of Daphne's book *A World Apart*. The party went well and there was no hint of the storm to come.

No doubt I should have anticipated the hostility that Daphne's book would provoke. She had shown me the typescript and although I had not read it all, I had read enough to know that her references to life in single-sex boarding-schools would attract attention. The fact that what she had to say was true and had been said many times before did not make the references to homosexuals in the common room and Young Woodleys in the study corridor any less provocative. But I had been so steeped in controversy myself and had so little sympathy with the old-fashioned boarding-school that it never crossed my mind to suggest to Daphne that these passages should be omitted.

Though I was prepared for controversy, I was taken aback by the vehemence of the attacks on *A World Apart*, all the more so because the earlier indications had been that the book would be favourably received. The novelist, Susan Hill, who had been sent the book to review, had written to Daphne: 'I did so very much like and admire and enjoy it.' Once the book was published, hostility gathered momentum with a vengeance. Public school headmasters told the press how much they disapproved of the book, though it was clear that few of them had read it. One headmaster who had congratulated Daphne on the book changed his mind in public and condemned it. Another told the press that Daphne must have been 'unbalanced' to give such a distorted picture of boarding-school life. Literary critics attacked the book as though they had personal scores to settle. Anonymous letters arrived, one of which began: 'For a woman in your position to have written such an appalling load of titillating filth . . .'

Daphne also received many letters of support, particularly from those who knew that her descriptions of boarding-school life were not exaggerated. One headmaster wrote to her: 'You are right to say that any headmaster who says there's no bullying in his school is a rash man. In eleven years here, I have expelled three boys for bullying and in each case it took *too* long to expose them.'

I intercepted the anonymous letters but I could not protect Daphne from the public criticism. What raw nerve had the book touched? The days when people got excited about dormitory revelations had long since gone. It was over sixty years since Alec Waugh's novel, *The Loom of Youth*, which described in guarded terms his adolescent experiences at Sherborne, had caused a similar outcry. *A World Apart* was different in one important respect from all the previous revelations of public school life: it was written by a woman. The fact that she was a headmaster's wife fuelled the sense of outrage that some former public schoolboys felt. The headmaster's wife was supposed to dispense tea and cakes not write about 'Tea and Sympathy'.

Some of the anger directed at Daphne was intended for me. For those headmasters who ran remote and less fashionable establishments, it was infuriating that the Raes, so comfortably placed at Westminster, should rekindle parents' anxieties about what went on in boarding-schools.

If that had been all there was to it, we could have weathered the storm. Some governors and members of staff expressed concern that the book was harming Westminster's reputation, but most thought that it would be a nine-days' wonder. The pupils appeared to take no interest and the parents we consulted could not understand what all the fuss was about. But, a week after the book's publication, a new dimension to the crisis emerged. It was claimed that two short passages in the book were based on individuals who could be identified, including a member of the Westminster staff. That swung the focus of the criticism away from Daphne and on to me. If the governors and the common room believed that I had seen those passages in typescript, my position as headmaster would be untenable.

I was sure I had not seen them. My careless attitude to controversy did not extend to ignoring such an obvious danger to my career. But this was difficult to prove and I could tell that my friends on the staff and the governing body had their doubts. For several days, while the routine of school life continued, my future hung in the balance. I began to consider what sort of deal I could do with the governing body if enough of its members turned against me.

When the governing body met, Burke Trend came to sit beside me and asked after Daphne. It was typical of the man that he should show more concern for her welfare than for the crisis that was preoccupying his fellow governors, who stood talking quietly together before the meeting started. Daphne's book was not on the agenda; that was to be discussed at the end of the meeting after I had departed. What *had* appeared on the agenda at short notice was a new proposal that Westminster should join the Assisted Places Scheme. Whoever put that on the agenda had an excellent sense of timing. I spoke against the proposal as forcefully as I could but my arguments carried less weight because in the minds of some governors my future was uncertain. I was supported by Edward Carpenter and Burke Trend but the meeting decided by a narrow majority that Westminster should apply to join the Assisted Places Scheme. A policy that I had publicly opposed since its inception had now been accepted by the school of which I was headmaster. If I needed an opportunity to resign on a matter of principle rather than await the governors' verdict on Daphne's book, this was it. But I remained silent.

I have no doubt that those governors who opposed my regime thought that the combined effect of the row over Daphne's book and the vote in favour of the Assisted Places Scheme would be enough to force me to resign. They wanted a different Westminster and I stood in their way. I do not think they planned a coup; they saw an opportunity and took it.

In the evening after the governing-body meeting, I went round to the Deanery. Edward and I collected the whisky bottle and two glasses from the dining room and went upstairs to his study. He told me that the governors had discussed the implications of Daphne's book for a long time and had not even considered whether they should ask me to resign. They did think, however, that 'in all the circumstances' it would be wise of me to look for another job sometime in the next two years. It was not an ultimatum, just advice. By 1985, I would have been at Westminster for fifteen years and that was probably time to be moving on. Meanwhile, the governors had confidence in me and would make that clear to the staff.

I plunged back into the job with renewed energy. The one thing I could not afford was to give the impression that I was a spent force. Authority soon deserts a headmaster who is thought to have lost his will to govern. But my eagerness to reaffirm my authority created its own hazards.

Two boys are sent to me for misbehaving in HP's class. He is an American exchange teacher and does not know how to control Westminster's tearaways. I have already warned that any more boys sent to me from that class will be dealt with severely. When the two boys arrive, I recognize one as a persistent nuisance who deserves to be sent home. Instead of inquiring what happened, I rusticate them both for a week. Later, I am told that the second boy had not been misbehaving; he only came along to support his friend. Blast! I will have to climb down in his case just at the time when I am trying to present to the school and the common room a calm, unflustered face. After all these years, how could I have made such an elementary mistake?

The rhythm of school life soon reasserted itself. Most of the staff were relieved that the crisis was over. Most of the pupils did not realize there had been one. The term wound its way through the longest hot summer of the century. Exam candidates wilted in the heat. Exhausted masters discovered matters of principle in the most trivial incidents. When tempers were well and truly frayed, two boys made a hoax bomb telephone call to the police during afternoon school and the buildings were suddenly overrun with alsatians. I counted the days until the end of term.

The governing body always met on the last day. When the main business was over, one of the governors who thought I should have resigned earlier in the term made a long complaint about the poor impression the pupils gave to outsiders: the boys were walking round Dean's Yard with their shirt-tails hanging out; the nonchalant attitude of the cricket XI had been adversely commented on by visiting teams; four-letter words had been heard in the cloisters. As soon as he had finished, two other governors came in quickly to contribute corroborating evidence. It had obviously been planned in advance.

It was, I think, the first time in thirteen years that the governors had raised the question of discipline. I had from time to time tried to interest them in the more serious issues such as the use of illegal drugs and stealing but they had shown no appetite for discussing them. Discipline was the headmaster's responsibility. So I was angry that these three governors should spring such disciplinary trivia on me at the end of a governing-body meeting.

But I understood their motives. They wanted to keep my departure on the agenda.

Later in the day, I thought of any number of withering responses – 'If the governors found a Westminster boy dying of an overdose of drugs they would tell him to tuck his shirt in' – but at the time I said only that if governors had complaints about the pupils' attitude and behaviour they should contact me direct. On this occasion it worked, though I had little doubt that like the Indians in my favourite western films the hostile governors would soon renew their attack. That they wanted me out was confirmed shortly after, when one of them told a friend of ours at a dinner aparty: 'We must get rid of John Rae.'

There is a lot to be said for a real threat in preference to a vague anxiety. Whereas, in the past, I had worried unnecessarily that I would lose the governors' confidence, now that I was certain I had lost it, at least in respect of these three, I felt relieved. I knew who my enemies were and looked forward to outmanoeuvring them until I had found another job. But my position was not as strong as I would have liked. In January 1984, Westminster's formal application to join the Assisted Places Scheme was made public. The press not unnaturally wanted to know whether I was going to continue as headmaster. The *Daily Telegraph* reported:

Last night, there was speculation about Dr Rae's future at the school which he has run for thirteen years, after such a disagreement with the governors. But the Very Rev. Dr Edward Carpenter, Dean of Westminster and chairman of the governors, said the suggestion of Dr Rae's resignation was 'lunatic, absolutely ridiculous.'

Edward, perhaps, protested too much. Burke Trend, to whom I had turned for advice on what to say to the press, used his drafting skills to produce a more measured statement:

'I have always had doubts about the Assisted Places Scheme and I still have them,' I told any journalists who called. 'The governors have decided on a limited experiment in our preparatory school, and I'm very happy to see how that experiment works out in practice.'

When I saw Neil Kinnock, a few days later, he said: 'I'm sorry we didn't have a chance to scrap the Assisted Places Scheme before you got hooked.'

I was not hooked on the scheme and never would be, but I sometimes wondered whether my very public opposition to it had been a miscalculation or, worse, a self-indulgence. That the scheme was bad I had no doubt, but I had been wrong in thinking that it would sour relations between the independent schools and the state schools. Once the scheme was up and running, it ceased to be a contentious issue and as long as there was a Conservative government, its future was assured.

Once again I had quickly to dispel any rumours that I was thinking of resigning. In the common room, as on the governing body, there were men who would have been glad to see me go. Every headmaster has his enemies on the staff, though enemies is too strong a word since most of the time they are no more than what the Duke of Wellington called 'croakers' – those who find fault with every decision. As long as the croakers confined themselves to croaking and moaning below decks I could ignore them, but if their disaffection was translated into intrigue they would be dangerous.

That is what happened. Under the impression that I had been fatally wounded by the events of the past year, the croakers thought they could deliver the *coup de grâce*. They had been excluded from favour by me and, not unnaturally, thought they would obtain preferment under a new headmaster. I tried to persuade myself that their antics were more of a nuisance than a threat but I knew that was not true. They had little support among the other members of staff but, like a disruptive minority who are determined to make life difficult for a teacher, they were capable of undermining my authority if I was not seen to be able to control them.

Their tactics were to embarrass me on those public occasions, such as the announcements in break on Monday mornings, when the whole staff was gathered together. When I had made my announcements, one of them would ask a question designed to put me on the defensive. 'Headmaster, has any decision been made about . . . ?' Another croaker would follow, directing his question, not at me, but at his fellow conspirator. 'Am I not right in thinking that we were assured that a decision would be made by today?'

How childish it all seems in retrospect, how easy it is to imagine that all I had to do was tell them to shut up. But they chose their subjects carefully, so that an angry or dismissive response would have sounded not strong but petulant. I did not want to lose face or be drawn into a public wrangle so I tried to give a calm reply, though there were times when my heart was racing and I had to speak slowly to avoid revealing that I was nervous.

My aim was to retain the initiative at all costs. I had no intention of being hustled into a premature resignation by an unrepresent-ative group of governors and masters. I would resign before the two years were up but I would choose the moment. In the meantime, I would conduct a fighting retreat, running the school, looking for another job, scanning the horizon for hostile governors and keeping one step ahead of the croakers. I made a point of writing more articles for the newspapers and of accepting invitations to take part in radio and television programmes because I reckoned that the more I was in the public eye the safer I would be. But it was the day-to-day management of the school that mattered; as long as I avoided making mistakes, getting on with the job was the best way of keeping the initiative.

The croakers were not well organized but they were quick to exploit situations. When some members of staff raised the well-worn issue of abolishing Saturday morning school, I was surprised to find that, on this occasion, the proposal had the support of a large majority in the common room. The croakers knew I was against abolition: Westminster still had far too many boarders for me to contemplate a five-day week. They also knew that the gov-ernors would be against a move that would effectively turn West-minster into a day school.

If I had been writing a handbook on strategy for headmasters, this was the situation I should have urged them to avoid: a proposal for change supported by the majority of the staff and opposed by the headmaster and the governing body. I made matters worse by trying to take an evenhanded approach between the abolitionists and their opponents, which only served to encourage the former and undermine the resolve of those with whom I was in sympathy. In the end, I told the staff that having listened to all the arguments I had decided that while I was headmaster Saturday morning school would remain. By then, the discussions had dragged on for nearly two terms and my handling of the issue was criticized even by my friends.

Towards the end of the summer term in 1984, Burke Trend warned me that the hostile governors were planning another attack. We considered how best to respond without – as he put it – 'leaving too much blood on the floor'. When the attack came at the July meeting of the governing body, it was on the now familiar theme of shirt-tails, bad language and bad manners. The minority had collected one or two new supporters but the debate ended inconclusively with Burke suggesting (as planned) that a small group of governors should meet with the headmaster to discuss the matter in the new school year.

By recording the skirmishes in this way, I may have given the impression that during my last two years at Westminster I was preoccupied with outmanoeuvring my critics but this was not the case. The trials of strength came and went and in between I was on good terms with most of those who seemed anxious to accelerate my departure. The trials took their toll, nevertheless, and, combined with those other disorientating experiences, encouraged me to consider the attractions of leading quite a different life. For thirty years, I had been a schoolmaster. It had been a good life but I had never given another career a chance and I wanted to prove to myself that I could succeed away from the familiar world of the public schools. I consulted head hunters who made optimistic noises but clearly saw me as a difficult person to place. 'Don't sell yourself short,' one of them told me, 'the right job for you is out there somewhere and it is worth waiting for.' I was not convinced. Nor was I sure that I wanted to wait. I toyed with politics and was accepted on to the SDP's list of candidates but my heart was not in it. Perhaps the best course after all would be to resign with as much favourable publicity as possible in the hope that someone would say, 'That's just the man we need . . .'

In the winter term of 1984, some of my zest for headmastering seemed to have gone. I had no more reforms to introduce. Reading a biography of A. J. Balfour, I came across a phrase that Balfour had used to describe a society in decline – 'the ship rises less buoyantly to each succeeding wave' – and noted it in my journal. After fourteen years, I needed a new challenge.

In the spring term of 1985, I resigned. I gave the governing body the required three terms' notice, which meant that I had a year to find a job. With the help of journalists who had been friends over the years, I let it be known that I was on the market, but there was no great rush for my services. People said: 'You're bound to get something.' Tantalizing possibilities appeared and then faded. When the head of a public relations company said, 'We mustn't be selfish and keep you to ourselves', I got the message. I began to think that I would have to fall back on writing, never a very profitable occupation as far as I was concerned, when a Westminster parent came to my rescue.

John Winter was a senior executive of Laura Ashley. Bernard and Laura Ashley wanted to set up a charitable foundation, one of whose aims would be to foster a second chance in education for those who had left school early or without qualifications. Was I interested in being the first director of the foundation? It was almost too good to be true, a chance to use someone else's money to demonstrate that the decisions of the education system were never final. I met Bernard and Laura Ashley. They had both left school in the sixth form and were wary of headmasters but we got on well enough and agreed terms. The foundation was already set up and generously funded. I would take over as soon as I left Westminster in March 1986. The croakers and the hostile governors had been outmanoeuvred; I had kept the initiative and found a job.

With my future settled, some of the old zest for the job returned but, if I had imagined that my final year at Westminster would be easy, I was soon disillusioned. The life of a school does not slow down because there is going to be a change of headmaster. The pupils, in particular, are unimpressed by what the headmaster may think of as the end of an era. Their interest in the change is strictly practical: will the new man be easier on drugs? Will he do something about the food? Meanwhile, they kick over the traces as they have always done.

My sense of what mattered and what didn't in their behaviour had not changed since I started at Westminster. At the end of my last summer term, I noted this in my journal:

I go for an early morning swim at the RAC in Pall Mall. In Birdcage Walk, I pass three Westminster boys returning to school, looking tired and unshaven. They are all leavers and have probably been out all night celebrating. No action needed. They are almost in their last day. They can look after themselves and have done no harm to the school. Why fuss? It is the pushers, thieves and vandals who require a strict arrest.

My conviction that Westminster had to find more space if it was going to compete successfully with schools such as Eton and St Paul's had not changed either. For a long time, I had been pressing the governors to buy a substantial building close to the school. We had our eye on an office block off Smith Square within easy walk of Dean's Yard. The plan was to convert it into the most modern science block in the country and to adapt the old science block for those subjects and activities that had previously had to move from space to space like a travelling circus.

The project would cost between three and four million pounds and, although the school was not poor, that sum could only be raised by a combination of borrowing and appealing for funds. Some governors were frightened by the scale of the operation, but I had left them little choice. I had increased the numbers to such an extent that, unless the governors bought the building, the quality of education Westminster offered was bound to deteriorate. I had a strong ally, too, in the new chairman of the executive committee, Gordon Pirie, who had no patience with his faint-hearted colleagues. At last, a few months before I left, the governors decided to buy. It was a bold decision and one that helped to ensure that the school would remain competitive. The task of raising the money was taken on by Lord Carr and by the development officer, Neil Mackay. I was their hit man. They set up meetings and I went to collect. In a city boardroom, I sat alone with a chairman whose son was in the sixth form. He asked me how much I wanted him to give. 'You must have some figure in mind,' he insisted. But I did not. Off the top of my head, I mentioned a large sum. He took out a cheque book, wrote the cheque and pushed it across the table. I had the impression that if I had added a nought, his response would have been exactly the same.

At the beginning of my last term, I had to appoint a new captain of the school. The choice lay between the boy who was head of College and a girl, Lynda Stuart. It was heartbreaking to see how much the boy wanted the position, but I was sure that Lynda would do a better job. The fact that she would be the first female head of school in four hundred and fifty years would attract some comment, as would the fact that she was black. Her family came from Barbados and her father was medical adviser to the Commonwealth Secretariat. I discussed with Lynda the possibility that some people might be critical of the appointment but she brushed my fears aside. She did not want publicity but if it came she would handle it herself. In the event, the few public comments on her appointment were favourable and I received only one hostile letter. The writer of the letter had been a boy at Westminster in the 1930s. 'Appointing a black girl as captain of the school,' he wrote, 'is a gross distortion of the natural order of things. It is wholly inappropriate.' It was a voice from the past, not from the vigorous, idiosyncratic Westminster of the eighteenth century but from a different strain in the school's tradition – snobbish, conventional and precious – the last traces of which I had tried to wipe out.

None of which worried Lynda at all; she was a successful captain, commanding respect without difficulty. I wondered then, as I had done often in the past, how these mature eighteen-year-olds managed to adapt themselves to a school regime that was designed for adolescents. And what did they think of us, the adults who had chosen to spend our lives telling (or not telling) the adolescents to tuck their shirt-tails in? I am not sure whether the constant company of the young preserves in teachers some of the characteristics of adolescence or whether it is the persistence of a youthful outlook which encourages teachers to seek the company of the young. Whichever it is, there is a touch of immaturity in many good teachers and rather more than a touch in many bad ones, so much so that it is part of a headmaster's role to ask the more mature pupils to be patient and understanding with the immature teachers, particularly when the latter are no longer young.

If a school is judged by the maturity of its pupils, Westminster would be reckoned one of the best, but if the yardstick is humility or godliness, I would be less confident of Westminster's pre-eminence. I did not give these qualities much emphasis and this was one of the underlying causes of the conflict between some of the governors and myself. I did not think it was a headmaster's job to try to make his pupils saints but rather to curb their natural inclination to be sinners. My hero among public school headmasters was not the celebrated Dr Arnold but his near-contemporary, Dr Keate, the headmaster of Eton from 1809 to 1834. Keate's reputation as a flogger – it is calculated that he flogged an average of ten boys a day – has distracted attention from the fact that he encouraged far greater intellectual freedom than Dr Arnold and his disciples. Unlike Arnold, Keate accepted the reality of boyhood and, unlike Arnold, he flogged boys to keep them in order not because he thought he could make them good. In a moment of hysteria, Arnold gave a boy eighteen strokes because he thought the boy was lying. When he discovered his mistake, Arnold apologized – but Keate would never have fallen into the trap of confusing righteous indignation with school discipline. Nor would I. When Westminster pupils lied, cheated and stole, I punished them to discourage others, not because I equated adolescence misdemeanour with sin. In other words, my approach to head-mastering was strongly influenced by my belief in the unimport-ance of adolescence. How pupils behaved, what their attitudes were, what causes they espoused, bore little or no relation to what sort of adults they would become. The child might be father of the man but the adolescent most definitely was not. That did not mean that I ignored or condoned their wrongdoing but that I refused to regard it as predictive of the future. It did not amount to a philosophy of education – heaven forbid – but it was the rough and ready yardstick by which I decided what mattered and what did not. As with our own children, I reckoned that, regardless of what they did between the ages of thirteen and eighteen, all these pupils would come good in their own time, and that for the few who made a mess of their lives, the roots lay much deeper than adolescence in the circumstances of childhood or the distribution of genes.

One of the final tasks of a departing despot is to secure his reputation. The governors had engaged an artist to paint my portrait. He produced a good likeness but the impression given to the spectator was of a relaxed man who was happy to leave the running of the school to others. So I asked him to make the face more haggard, to darken the shadows under the eyes and generally to indicate the stress and strain of the job. Satisfied with the result, I chose a suitable place for the portrait to hang, hoping that my successor would not move it to some obscure corner as incoming headmasters had been known to do.

A more serious threat to my reputation was presented by a proposed new history of the school. A former housemaster, whose early retirement from his house I had done nothing to impede, had already submitted a first draft, in which he had managed to describe my sixteen years as headmaster mentioning my name only once. I felt under no obligation to recommend to the governors that this curiosity should be published. Instead, I persuaded them to commission John Field, who was then librarian and archivist, to write a more balanced version of events. Field would not take a flattering view of my stewardship but he was sympathetic to what I had been trying to do at Westminster and I was happy to leave history in his hands. His book, *The King's Nurseries*, was published in 1987.

Having done my best to put the record straight, I was ready to go. A few weeks before I left, Edward Carpenter retired from the Deanery. I invited him to Latin Prayers to beg a play. Though the school knew him only by sight and knew nothing of the battles he and I had fought against those governors who had tried to bring Westminster's non-conformity to heel, the prospect of an additional half-holiday ensured that they listened to him with good humour. He spoke at length, touching on a number of his favourite philosophical themes, while I remained seated on the low dais, shifting my gaze, watchful and reflective, from row to row, and wondering whether a pigeon would appear.

When Edward had finished, the school applauded and I

announced the psalm. The pupils stood and sang lustily, 'Ad te levavi oculos meos, qui habitas in coelis'. It was not a religious occasion, more a tribal rite. The Latin spoke of lifting eyes to heaven but the cheerfully defiant voices of the young suggested a more down to earth theme: 'Deans and headmasters come and go but we go on for ever.'

EPILOGUE

The portrait of the public school headmaster as an absolute ruler of his little kingdom is a caricature but a recognizable one. Until the Second World War, my predecessors at Westminster were greeted at the first night of the annual Latin Play with Handel's 'See, the conquering hero comes'. The war gave the kiss of death to numerous dotty public school customs, including that one, but the public school headmaster is still expected to play the king in a way that is not really true of any other job I can think of, and when he retires, he is a king without a country. Like ex-King Zog of Albania who used to appear at our suburban house during the war to be X-rayed by my father, the ex-headmaster has about him an almost visible sense of loss. A sense of loss may also invade his dreams. When I left Westminster, I had this recurring dream: I am a headmaster again, not of Westminster but of a smaller and less well-known school, and as I wander disconsolately about the ill-kept campus and dingy buildings, I tell myself that I must have been mad to exchange one of the best jobs in the business for exile in this obscure, provincial outpost.

But that was all. I experienced no other withdrawal symptoms and in my waking hours I was unaware of any sense of loss. I had enjoyed being a headmaster but the last thing I wanted was to go back. Whatever delusions of grandeur went with the job I was happy to forego. I was a free man and a private citizen. At the invitation of 'Tiny' Rowland, I joined the board of the *Observer* newspaper and was pleased to discover that the directors operated as school governors should but seldom do, deciding strategy but not trying to interfere in the day-to-day running of the paper. For two years, I was Professor of Rhetoric at Gresham College, London, a post that had been held by one of my heroes, Robert Birley, after he had left Eton, and that our children, under the impression that rhetoric was a Greek word for talking the hind legs off a horse, thought I was well qualified to fill. I chuckled when I received communications addressed to 'Professor Rae' and spent the modest stipend with Daphne on a room with a view in a convent overlooking Florence. The duties were not onerous. I gave six lunchtime lectures a year in the church of St Mary Le Bow and seized the opportunity to explain to the audience who had drifted in – city gents, tourists trapped unawares, the odd tramp sheltering from the wind in Cheapside – what was wrong with British education.

I had more time for the family. Rather late in the day, some of them may have thought; they did not now have to compete with other people's children for my attention, but they were no longer children themselves. They had come good in their own time, defying the pessimistic forecasts of their early teachers and demonstrating, once again, how unwise it is to judge children's potential on their performance at a young age. While I rejoice in their academic achievements, what gives Daphne and me much greater pleasure is that, despite the hazards of being the headmaster's children, they have become such mature and likeable adults. And now that their own children are of school age, I am happy to be drawn back into those discussions that go on in families all over the world, about good schools and bad schools, and why they should be so; and when the conversation moves, as it inevitably does, to the merits and demerits of a particular school, its reputation for academic excellence or moral depravity, Siobhan turns to me and asks, 'What is the headmaster like? Is he any good?'

My departure from Westminster and my undemanding duties as director of the Laura Ashley Foundation also gave me the freedom and opportunity to write. In the first three years, I published two books and so many articles that my critics, who had followed my career with increasing irritation and who must have thought that when I ceased to be a headmaster they had heard the last of me, were exasperated to find when they opened their newspapers that the reports of my disappearance had been exaggerated. In 1987, I was writing a fortnightly column in *The Times* and one almost as frequently in the London *Evening Standard*, as well as occasional articles in other papers. I confess to deriving some pleasure from returning to haunt those who had been glad to see the back of me but my reasons for plungeing into journalism were more substantial. It paid well and it enabled me to take part in the lively debate that preceded the introduction of Kenneth Baker's Education Act of 1988.

Meanwhile the work of the Laura Ashley Foundation turned my thoughts still further away from public schools. Since one of the aims of the Foundation was to give a second chance to adults who had left school with few or no qualifications, I encountered at first hand individuals who were the casualties of Britain's elitist, many-are-called-but-few-are-chosen philosophy of education. They had been written off at the age of sixteen or even at the age of eleven and here they were asking the Foundation for a grant to study at university. Like a handful of survivors who had managed to swim ashore against all the odds, they told the true story of just how much talent had been lost.

Much of my writing in these years was on the theme of wasted talent. It was not an original theme but I embraced it with the zeal of a convert. The British persisted with an education system that attempted to divide pupils at the age of sixteen into those who had the potential to go far and those who did not, the former taking A level to qualify for university, the latter leaving school to swell the ranks of an under-educated work force. It was the old officer and other ranks mentality in a different guise. Quite apart from the waste of individual talent, economic prosperity in the modern world obviously depended on a well-educated population not just on a well-educated elite.

It was easy to theorize from the sidelines, something I had criticized others for doing in the past, and I was aware that I was skating on thin ice, not only because I had no direct experience of the state schools but also because I had been headmaster of one of the most elitist schools in the country. But I was convinced that I was right: it was the officers and other ranks mentality that prevented Britain developing as good an education system as its competitors. So when we wring our hands, as we shall, I believe, for many years to come over our failure to give all our children a good education, we should remember that the reason is not progressive teaching methods or lack of resources, but our unspoken national conviction that most children are not worth giving a good education to. They are, after all, only going to become other ranks.

On this note, my public involvement in the education debate ended. Though I continued to contribute the occasional article to the newspapers, the prolific period of writing that had followed my departure from Westminster was over. In 1989, I approached one of the head hunters who had given me helpful advice in the past. I had run the Laura Ashley Foundation for three years and, while its central theme had interested me very much, the work was not sufficiently demanding. When people asked, 'Is that a full-time job?' I became depressed. I was only fifty-eight and not ready to become a part-timer. The head hunter said that he did not think he had anything that would suit me; the alcoholic drinks industry was looking for someone to run a new organization, provisionally called the Alcohol Industry Council, but that hardly sounded the sort of job for a former public school headmaster. I agreed, but said that since I was there we might as well talk about what the job entailed. Half an hour later, I was hooked.

The drinks industry saw itself threatened by the possibility of restrictions on its freedom to promote and sell its products; public awareness of the health risks of excessive consumption and public disquiet about lager louts and drunken drivers had created a climate in which measures such as a ban on alcohol advertising might command popular support. The job of the Alcohol Industry Council, or the Portman Group as it soon became (because it had first met in Portman Square), would be to promote sensible drinking and to combat alcohol misuse. If the industry itself took an active part in reducing alcohol problems, the threat of restrictions on commercial freedom could be headed off, if not for ever, then at least for long enough to enable the industry to diversify its interests.

The contradictory nature of the job and the difficulty of giving teeth to a role that many people would regard as a public relations exercise, appealed to me. Perhaps most of all, I was excited at the prospect of working for the commercial sector. In the past, public school headmasters had gone on to become bishops or heads of Oxford or Cambridge colleges, to run charities or to help banks with graduate recruiting, but never to enter the real commercial world of selling goods, of trade, which many academics still regarded with suspicion and distaste. I had no qualms. The men who ran the drinks industry were frank about what they hoped to achieve and so was I. They wanted to protect their industry and thought that reducing alcohol misuse was one way of doing so; I thought that society would be a better place if fewer people drank too much and was happy if in tackling this issue I helped to protect the industry. That there would be times when the industry and I disagreed, we all understood from the start.

In September 1989, I became the first director of the Portman Group, a position that I still hold and that has proved as complex and stimulating as I could have wished. Like headmastering, it sometimes keeps me awake at night, but unlike headmastering, it is a job not a way of life. I enjoy rubbing shoulders with the commercial world; the men and women I work for are refreshingly free from the prickliness, the determination to take criticism personally and the gift for losing all sense of proportion that made some, but by no means all, schoolteachers so hard to live with. We disagree but it is never personal. They give and take hard knocks but are seldom petty. I am not idealizing the commercial world, which has its warts, just noting its contrast with the academic world I have left behind.

One particular contrast gives me an uneasy conscience. Though I may regret having had to dismiss members of staff, I do not believe that I was wrong to do so. What troubles my conscience is the memory of the members of staff I failed to dismiss. The commercial world cannot afford to tolerate incompetence, but the academic world allows those whose performance is inadequate – university lecturers who cannot lecture, schoolteachers who cannot teach – to remain in their posts. I allowed one or two men to remain at Westminster whom I knew to be incompetent or disloyal or both. It was not because I had scruples – I have yet to meet a public school headmaster who was not unscrupulous when it suited him –

but because in these cases I was anxious to avoid antagonizing public opinion.

This anxiety is the key to understanding the role of the public school headmaster: why he appears to be both callous and vacillating; why for all his talk of consultation he still adopts an autocratic style of government; why he is a thoroughly modern manager one moment and a charismatic leader the next; why despite the Christian context of his appointment he behaves as a disciple of 'Machiavelli anticristo'. The contradictions reflect the central paradox of his position: while he wields power to an unusual degree over the lives of others, he is seldom secure himself. Not that he can ever give the slightest hint that he is insecure, because his authority depends on everyone believing that he is the opposite.

In my own case, insecurity was heightened by echoes of childhood and by my determination to prove I could do the job despite my modest paper qualifications, but that does not alter the fact that the central paradox is true for all public school headmasters, indeed for the heads of comparable independent schools wherever they may be. As it says in the epigraph, 'The ever-present fact of life for the head is that he or she is vulnerable, a condition not conducive to peace of mind or relaxation.' Being vulnerable may lead the head to play safe or take risks, but the one thing he cannot afford to do is to lose the initiative to the staff or the pupils or the parents. He is the captain of the ship and he must be in control. His survival depends on it.

To see headmastering solely in these terms is to ignore the complexity of human motivation. Although all public school heads are driven, I believe, by this perceived link between success and survival and by the need to stay one step ahead of their critics, each brings to the job his or her own agenda of experience and ideas. My own agenda was unsophisticated. I did not have a philosophy of education and I found the literature on educational theory boring. I had enjoyed the life of a schoolmaster at Harrow and I knew the difference between a good school and a bad one. I was probably more at home with the Artful Dodgers than the Oliver Twists but I was also too much of a poacher turned gamekeeper to make the mistake my own headmaster had made, of allowing boys to remain who should have been expelled. I had no grand design but I left

Westminster a more successful school than I found it. And it was fun.

I realize that people thought I was lucky to be appointed to Westminster. At any other time than 1970, when the young appeared to have seized the initiative from their elders, the governors would surely have insisted on appointing a headmaster in the traditional – classical scholar, clerical collar – Westminster mould. But I am not sure whether I believe in luck. I used to discuss it with my sixth form when we needed a break from Napoleon's campaigns and I would tell again the story of how the Emperor, when an officer was recommended to him for high command, asked, 'Is he lucky?'

In the summer of 1991, when I went to see a cancer specialist, I was reminded of those pleasant diversions from the syllabus. I had noticed what looked like a dark, irregular-shaped mole high on my back. As there had been publicity about a particularly evil form of skin cancer called a melanoma, I immediately assumed the worst, but my hypochondria had cried wolf so often I was reluctant to give in too easily to those familiar fears. When, after a suitable interval to assure myself that the hypochondria had gone at last, I saw a skin specialist, he told me without a moment's hesitation that the mole was cancerous. He did not say what he thought of my prospects but the speed with which he sent his bill was not encouraging.

The cancer specialist, Meirion Thomas, was one of those doctors who believe in treating their patients as intelligent adults. He explained the situation to me. He would remove the melanoma under a local anaesthetic. The chances of the cancer recurring were directly related to the thickness of the mole. In 1970, an American physician, Alexander Breslow, had discovered that if the melanoma was less than 1.5 millimetres thick, the chances of the cancer recurring were small. The laboratory would give us the answer in a few days.

My melanoma turned out to be 1.2 millimetres thick. Meirion tells me that while there can be no guarantee that the cancer will not recur, I shall be very unlucky if it does. That raises an interesting question. Will the fact that I have been so lucky in life work in my favour now or against? To have had with Daphne a large and happy family, to have been the headmaster of a great school, to have written what I wanted to write and, then, when other headmasters are contemplating retirement, to have stumbled upon a stimulating job in the commercial world, is to have been lucky indeed. So that if one day my luck runs out, though I shall find that difficult to accept, I shall hardly have cause to complain.

I go to see Meirion every two to three months for a check up. He has a son at Westminster, and was himself educated at one of those excellent Welsh grammar schools that took the children of the valleys and lifted their eyes to the hills. More often than not, when we meet our thoughts turn to education. Meirion would like to take time off to teach in the medical school at Vellore in India, the same medical school that Manjur, the boy who corrected my grammar in the leprosy village at Sunderpore, is hoping to attend. Manjur came top of the school-leaving exam in Raxaul, the nearby town. In Raxaul, as in other parts of Bihar, marks are a purchasable commodity – local politicians and officials buy marks for their children – so Manjur did well to reach the top on his own merits. He wants to be a doctor and, when he is qualified, to work with leprosy patients. His headmaster, Mr Rahindra, who bore himself with dignity and held the chalk between the stumps of his fingers, had been right to have such high hopes. What is the point of being a teacher if you do not believe in your pupils?

INDEX